How to Find a Lost Dog

How to Find a Lost Dog

The Pet Owner's Guide

Karin TarQwyn

Although the standard protocol is to thank human mentors, I must thank two of the most remarkable canines to have ever graced planet Earth.

Dedication to Cade:

You have taught me more than any human, animal, or angel I have ever encountered.

You know more about missing dogs than anyone ever has or ever will. I thank the universe every day that I met you that cold spring day in 2005. You have been the mentor we all look for in life.

Thank you, Cade.

Dedication to Paco:

When you came into my life as an eight-week-old puppy, I could never have imagined how important and influential you would be in my life. You have helped train oodles of tracking dogs as our token lost dog, but more importantly, you have been the little general I could always count on. You have been the most "pawsative" influence in my life, and I have gained strength from your unceasing loyalty. See you at the bridge, my friend.

To all the pet owners and dogs who have crossed my path, you have helped shape what became for me a passion and then a career.

Thank you.

About the Author

At the age of seven, when other little girls were playing with Barbies and baby dolls, Karin Chockley was in her backyard pretending she and her trusty crossbreed, Ace, were performing in obedience trials at Madison Square Garden. By third grade, she had memorized all the breeds in the American Kennel Club registry, and Ace could adeptly perform all the required tasks to earn a CDX title. But alas, he was a mutt, and she was just eight years old. Her love of dogs and dreams of working with them would fascinate her past childhood and into life as an adult.

The dream would become a reality when Karin began her training in private investigations in 1996 never realizing that dogs and work as a private investigator were about to collide. In 1997, she had the opportunity to train and work with search and rescue K9 units in the California Rescue Dog Association (CARDA). "The partnership with a dog and excitement of helping others was a dream come true for me," she explains. "I was hooked from the first day and found myself out looking for a dog to train for search and rescue work the next weekend." Over the next five years, Karin trained and handled two search dogs, both trained to trail human scent over long distances.

In 2002, after returning to Oklahoma and purchasing a ranch, she experienced a loss that would forever change her life: a beloved canine friend, Jack, went missing. The overwhelming grief was made worse by the fact that she could find no fact based system in place to find him—no proven techniques, equipment, or avenues to strategically pursue a missing pet.

In 2004, Karin decided to find missing pets full-time, forgoing any other type of investigations. Through continuous self-study as well as seminars and research, she has honed her skills in behavior and missing-pet scenario profiling.

When in her home state of Nebraska, a large percentage of her work is done over the phone profiling and designing recovery strategies for pet owners. The rest of her time is spent on the road with her crew of canines traveling the country and helping pet owners find their lost and missing four-pawed family members.
For additional information about Karin, visit http://k9pi.com/about_karin.html.

Do not go where the path may lead,
go instead where there is no path
and leave a trail.

—RALPH WALDO EMERSON

Contents

About the Author · vii
From Karin · xiii

Section 1: Getting Started · **1**
How to Use This Guide and Companion Website · 3
Cautionary Tales—Scams and the Missing Pet · 5
Behavior Basics—Interaction and Reaction · 12

Section 2: The Nine Scenarios: Profiling, Analysis and Strategies · · · · · · · · · · · · · · **17**
Introduction To The Nine Scenarios · 19
The Dog That Is Found by a Citizen · 20
The Roaming Dog · 26
The Stolen Dog · 35
The Dog That Meets with an Accident · 43
The Dog Experiencing Confusion, Illness, or Pain (CIP) · · · · · · · · · · · · · · · · 48
The Dog That Is Accidentally Transported · 54
The Dog That Is Intentionally Displaced or Removed · · · · · · · · · · · · · · · · · · 58
The Dog That Is Accidentally Trapped · 62
The Dog That Meets with a Predator · 66

Section 3: Actions, Activities, and Techniques · **71**
First-Response Protocol · 73
Ground-Zero Search · 76
How to Call for Your Dog · 78
How to Approach or, More Precisely, *Not* Approach the Roaming Dog · · · · · · · · 80
Notifying Emergency Animal Hospitals · 83
Developing Leads and Witnesses · 84

How to Handle Sightings · 87
Pet Identification Lineup Card · 92
Making the Rounds: Checking with Animal Shelters, Humane Societies, Animal Control, and Other
      Public Agencies · 94
Community-Awareness
      Campaign: Taking It to the Streets · 97
Automated Mass-Calling Systems · 103
Car Signs · 104
Flyers · 106
Place an Ad in the Local Newspaper · 108
Post on Websites · 110
Creating a Buzz with Social Media · 111
Involving the Media · 113
Investigative Field Techniques · 116
Spotlighting · 116
Tiger Line Physical Search · 118
Hire a Professional to Assist with Your Search · 119
Attraction, Surveillance, and Capture Techniques · · · · · · · · · · · · · · · · · 125
Encouraging Your Dog to Approach · 125
Using a Magnet or Lure Animal · 127
Associative-Response Conditioning · 129
Feeding-and-Comfort Stations · 131
Keeping out the Ants · 134
The Tuna Spritzer · 135
Surveillance and Monitoring · 137
The Humane Trap · 141
The Enclosure Trap · 146

Section 4: Home Sweet Home: What to Do after Your Pet Is Home · · · · · · · · · · · · **149**

Section 5: Prevention · **153**
The Most Common Ways in Which Dogs Go Missing · · · · · · · · · · · · · · · · 154

Section 6: References & Resources · **159**
Glossary · 161
Resources · 169
Acknowledgments · 171
About the Author · 173
Bibliography · 175

From Karin

First let me share… I have been in the place you are now.

   The purpose of this book is simple: to help pet owners focus on the right actions in the right places to find their missing dog faster. When my dog Jack went missing, it was truly the worst experience of my life. I was a private investigator and had also trained in the search and recovery of missing people. However, like most people experiencing a missing-dog crisis, I did not know what had happened to Jack or what would be the most effective way to find him. I put up flyers, walked and drove miles of fields and streets, but I did not receive the lead that would bring Jack home.

Today, I know the search for a missing dog goes beyond talking to people and driving around. The search for a missing dog must be performed based on what has actually happened to the pet.

Four and half months after Jack went missing, I was rewarded with the phone call that ended my search. Yes, Jack was found, and it is a story that rivals those of Lassie and *The Incredible Journey*. To read about Jack's great adventure, go to the companion website to this book at http://www.howtofindalostdog.org/losing-jack-and-finding-a-new-life.html.

Losing and finding Jack changed my life forever. Since 2005, I have dedicated my life working full-time in the location and recovery of missing dogs. Within this book are the profiling and processes I have developed and use in my investigative agency. The techniques and tasks are those I implement with my clients every day. With the purchase of this book, you also receive exclusive access to our companion website at www.howtofindalostdog.org where additional information, resources, instructions, updates, and new information can be found. You can also submit a query form about your missing dog on the site.

Read, scan, profile, follow the directions, and go to the website.
   With persistence and strategic action, you can find and recover your own missing dog.
   Here we go…

~Karin

Getting Started...

How to Use This Guide and Companion Website

This guide is set up for you to navigate quickly. I want to keep your reading to a minimum, so it is not necessary to read the whole guide.

The Behavior and Profiling Analysis by Scenario is found in section 2, "The Nine Scenarios." It is suggested you scan and answer the profiling query for each scenario before you read through the scenario.

All activities, actions, and techniques are found in section 3, "Actions, Activities, and Techniques." You will only need to read, understand, and do the actions suggested for your missing dog's probable scenario.

Aftercare and things to know once your dog is home are found in section 4, "Home Sweet Home."

A synopsis of the most common lost incidences and suggested techniques for prevention are found in section 5, "Prevention."

In section 6, "References and Resources," you will find a glossary of terms as well as other information related to the writing of this book.

Many of the scenarios and techniques are explained in further detail with photo displays on the website at http://www.howtofindalost-dog.org/.

To log in to the website, simply click on this photo, which is displayed prominently throughout the website.

Let's get started…

1. Read through the chapter "Cautionary Tales" so you are aware of some of the frauds and hoaxes that one can encounter while searching for a lost pet.
2. Next read "Behavior Basics." Many of the profiles are dependent on understanding and making a clear assessment of your dog's most probable behavior profile. The C4T, (Confident, Calm, Courageous, Cooperative, and Trusting of Humans), and STARS (Shy, Timid, Aloof, Reserved or Skittish), profiles are deciding factors in many scenarios.
3. Proceed to the "Nine Scenarios." Be sure to read through the queries for each scenario before reading through the entire scenario. If 50 percent of the questions on the queries are yes, this scenario is a possibility for your missing dog. Read and understand that scenario.
4. Read through each possible scenario, paying particular attention to those characteristics that appear to be the most like your dog or the escape event.
5. Read through the "Profile" section. This section describes the profile or behavioral characteristics of the pet most likely to experience this specific scenario. It also includes characteristics of the environment and surrounding area.
6. Next read through the "Characteristics, Sightings, and Leads." This information is typical for the subject scenario.
    Example: Your pet was last seen near a public park and has not been seen since, which is classic for a pet that has been rescued by a citizen. However, your dog is highly frightened of other people and most likely would not allow a stranger to approach. We are pursuing the most probable situation, so a frightened, skittish pet is most likely not going to allow itself to be rescued. Use your intuition and common sense.
7. Once you have reviewed the most likely scenarios, review and scan the activities in "Actions, Activities and Techniques." If you have more than one possible scenario, and many pet owners do, cross-reference the activities that may be the same for similar occurrences. Some activities will have more than one page; some will have less.
8. Begin your activities, taking those actions that relate to Community Awareness as your top priority.
9. As a purchaser of this book, you are eligible to participate in the companion website. The website includes additional tips, suggestions, and photos. Many of the techniques are explained in greater detail with additional photographic instructions. In addition, you can submit a query form about your lost dog and the missing event surrounding his disappearance.
10. To log in, simply click on the author's photo, which is prominent on the website. To submit a query form to Karin or a member of her staff, you will need your receipt # or date of purchase for this book.

Stay focused and diligent. You can do this.
Get started now.

Cautionary Tales—Scams and the Missing Pet

As we get started, it would be remiss of me if I did not caution you to some of the unfortunate situations that go on in the missing-pet world. I realize you are going through possibly one of the worst experiences of your life, but unfortunately, there are those who may try to take advantage of your grief and panic.

Years ago missing pets were not even on the scam artist's radar, but all that has changed with the increased reach of the Internet and social media. It is now common for heartbroken pet owners to receive calls, e-mails, and texts from scammers offering fraudulent services as well as saying they have found their lost pet. At the end of this chapter, please review the preventive techniques recommended to prevent you from becoming a victim.

Below are some of the most common scams pet owners are confronted with:

The Truck Driver or Vacationer Scam
Your dog has been found and is now supposedly a long distance away.

The caller states he or she is a truck driver and has found your dog while he or she was driving through your area. As the truck driver is on a time schedule, he or she had to keep driving and is now in a state or location far away. A twist on this scam is the vacationer who found your dog while on vacation and has now returned home. In both cases the finder wants you to wire or send money so he or she can fly or ship the dog back to you. The finder may also request money for boarding your dog or say the dog was injured and he or she needs to pay the vet bills. Regardless, this scammer has a story wherein your dog is a distance away and the person wants you to send money so he or she can get your dog back to you. Do not fall for it. The caller does not have your dog.

Reward Me in Advance
Some callers state they have found your dog and need you to pay the reward before they meet with you to return the dog. They may say their children are now in love with the dog and they have to buy another dog or that they have someone who wants to buy the dog. There are many different stories that are told, but the bottom line is the callers want the money up front before they give you your dog.

A twist on this scam is the partnered scam that plays out the same way but may have more than one player involved in the scam. The first caller states he or she has your dog and gathers information. After your informational response, the caller now says, "No, this is not your dog," and hangs up. A second scammer calls you later, saying he or she has found your pet. This caller has more information, and based on his or her recital of your missing pet's information, you are sure it is your dog. This scammer like the others wants to be paid in advance.

The Caller Needs to Buy Your Pet from Someone

The person calling or texting explains that they know where your dog is but they have to buy the dog back from the person who has the dog. They ask that you give them the money up front and they will then go to get your dog and meet up with you as soon as they have the dog. This is the scam that many people fall for as the caller pleads with them to do the right thing so he or she can go get their dog. The caller may even throw in added urgency frantically stating that the finder is going to sell the dog to a pit bull fighter for bait. The caller may plead if he or she can just get there before the sale, he or she is sure to buy the dog back. This is a scam. The caller has no idea where your dog is.

The Huge Reward

This scam can get very elaborate if you are offering a large reward. We have had pet owners offer up to $50,000 cash for the return of their pet. Once the reward amount is substantial, it may encourage the elaborate and more sophisticated scammers to get involved. There are many sketchy stories that can be told, including that the caller wants to meet you with your pet.

Pet owners must be careful when responding to calls when a large reward is offered. Even if the caller does not want to be paid up front and says he or she will meet you, caution is advised as a scammer can also turn into a thief or thug.

Case Study: Please note this was not our case at the time this scam was perpetrated.

From the pet owner:

"This is so sick I cannot believe this happened to me. A man responded to my CL post. He claimed his friend found my dog and that I should meet him.

I asked him to provide a description of the dog and to send a photo. He could not describe the dog and said he did not know how to take a picture with his phone.

Even though he is phone illiterate, he starts texting me. He will no longer answer his phone. He gives me a vague address, and I agree to meet him. I want my dog back, but this is really getting fishy, so I called my friend to go with me.

The texter now asks if I am coming alone, and I said no my husband is with me. He gives us a new address, and now I have called four other friends. This is all very hinky.

When we arrive at the address, we see a guy who walks quickly into an alley and asks in a text for me to follow him. I did not.

I was kind of freaked out by now, but still maybe this idiot has my dog? After an hour, it is clear this is a scam, and we left. We should probably never have gone there in the first place. The guy was a predator. I am smarter now, but people need to be cautious."

Susan S.—San Jose, California

Our Case Study:

Pico—Dallas, Texas

Pico was stolen from a doggie day care while the lobby of the facility was full of customers dropping off their dogs for the day. No one saw Pico disappear, and it was not discovered until our client went to pick him up to go home.

Our investigation began immediately. We began a large campaign with a substantial reward. This was a very industrial area, and there is a thriving drug culture operating in the area. We surmised that Pico was taken by an opportunist to make some quick money.

Three days after Pico was stolen, the pet owner received a call from a man who said, "he knew where Pico was but that he had to give the guy who had Pico some money because the guy was a drug addict and needed money right away." We had a huge campaign up by now with that large reward. My client called me and explained the situation. I told him not to give the guy any money but instead to tell him that he and his friends would go with him to get the dog and then give him the money. While I was on the phone, the scammer balked and said, "No, his friend was afraid of the cops, and no one could go." I again told my client that this was a scam; this guy had no idea where Pico was. I reminded him that the guy could not describe Pico beyond what was on the sign. I hung up the phone, convinced my client now understood that this helpful citizen was really on the take.

I got a call four hours later, and my client was crying. After I hung up the phone, the scammer had come back and agreed to let the group follow him as long as they stayed back several blocks so the guy who had their dog would not see them. Desperate, my client agreed and gave the guy a hundred dollars and began to follow the scammer as allowed. Within two blocks the guy slipped away down an alley, and they never saw him again.

Pico was recovered ten days later. The wonderful family that brought him back had bought him on a street corner for one hundred dollars the same day he was stolen. They loved the little Chihuahua, and he had become a member of their family. Two weeks after Pico had been abducted, a story about our search for Pico was on the evening news. The family had seen the news and recognized the dog in the story as the little dog they had bought two weeks earlier. They called and returned him refusing to take the reward or any reimbursement. Heartbroken, they gave my client all the beds, sweaters and things they had bought for Pico while he was living them. The family had been shocked to find that the cute little dog they bought from a woman at a convenience store had been stolen.

Pico had already been sold when the scammer contacted my clients saying he knew where the dog was. He did not. It is possible that he had stolen Pico himself, but that was never proven. The drug addict he was most likely talking about was himself.

Prevention—Do Not Become a Victim

Below are some of the preventive measures you can take to stay focused on your search and not be victimized by a scam artist.

Pictures speak a thousand words, and in this day and age of social media and cell phones, just about everyone has the ability to take a photo and text it or place it online.

Ask the caller to text or message you photos of the dog in his or her possession. The photo should be from the front so you can see the dog's face and identity. Most people will provide photos if they have your dog. If they tell you their phone is broken or they do not have a text function and the like, suggest they use a friend's phone. If they cannot do this, assume this is a scam and do not engage any longer.

Ask and do not tell

As the pet owner, your job is to collect information and not give it. So from the start of every conversation, make sure you ask the questions.

Do not describe your dog, where he went missing, or any of his habits, markings, or behaviors. Instead ask questions about the dog they have. Ask them to describe the dog. Ask them to describe any unique features they notice about the dog they have. Ask if they notice a collar or ID on the dog. Every dog has a unique identifier specific only to that dog. That unique identifier should not be made public as it will be one of the characteristics we use to determine the validity of sightings, leads, and statements. If the caller cannot provide any information other than what is on the sign or on social media, assume this is a scam.

Missing-Pet-Services Scams

Scammers calling to say they have your pet are not the only type of scams pet owners may encounter. There are now many different types of lost pet services out there, and not all of them are legitimate or reliable. Some service providers are diligent and provide a professional service, while others may do so some of the time but not always. Perhaps in no other field is the percentage of flimflam and incompetent service providers more prevalent than in the missing-pet arena.

Below are some of the more common service provider scams.

Lost pet finder services caller

You are called by a man or woman offering lost pet services for a small amount of money. The caller may or may not have a heavy accent. Many times these calls are coming from outside the United States, and the goal is to get your credit-card number. The caller will tell you one amount and then bill your card for more. The card number may then be sold and used by other racketeers to purchase items.

Tracking dog online

This is a website advertising search dogs or tracking dogs. There are photos of dogs in orange vests or dogs that look like police or military working dogs. The website encourages you to schedule a search dog in your area by filling out the form and paying the fee online. The K9 handler or the company will contact you to schedule your search upon payment. The amount for the up-front fee has been anywhere from $50.00 to $350.00. Once the amount is paid, the pet owner will never hear from the K9 handler and will be unable to get through on the phone line that is given on the website.

Additional services offer

The caller identifies him or herself as a staff member of a company you have actually engaged for some type of service. He or she asks if your pet is still missing and offers additional services to help. The person will ask for your credit-card information. This caller has obtained your contact information from a website or social media for lost pet services. The company you have engaged is legitimate; this caller is not. This scam is also set up to obtain your credit-card information.

Western Union dog tracker

These individuals or companies offer dog-tracking services but want you to send their fees up front to Western Union or a Walmart Cash Card. They may or may not show up, but there are never any results from this type of service.

The dog tracker or searcher says you cannot go with him or her on the search

Be cautious of anyone who says he or she will perform on-location work that you cannot be present for. This may not be so much an all-out scam but is the mark of an inexperienced and possibly less than honest individual. Over the years, dog trackers have come and gone, and many have not been so much scammers but delusional and inexperienced. For years, there was a guy who came out at midnight, telling the pet owner that he would work through the night and the next day. He would get back to them as soon as he had their pet. Most pet owners never heard from him again. In at least one case, he had left the search within three hours and went to another search that he had scheduled at the same time. Neither of these pet owners ever heard from the guy again.

Prevention and Best Practices

Guard the card—your credit or debit card
Do not give your card number to anyone without thoroughly checking out the credentials of the individual or company you intend to hire.

Offer to call the service provider back on the phone number on the website. All professionals will have a website you can go to and view stories and testimonials from their many successes.

Do not pay anyone for service without first talking with him or her
If they are professionals, they should go over your missing dog's situation with you before telling you how they can help.

Do not send money through Western Union or other cash-provider outlet
Professionals will have the ability to take PayPal as well as credit and debit cards. There is no recourse with cash outlets, especially those that are outside the United States.

Insist on going on the search for your pet with the on-location searcher or tracker. You have information that the searcher or investigator will need as they conduct the on location search.

Check references and testimonials
If they are professionals, they will have many clients who are happy to sing their praises. See the chapter in this book on hiring a professional in section 3 of this book for more good practices.

Do a Google search of the company or person you are considering hiring
If you put the key words *scam* or *complaint* behind their name in the search box, you should get any angry past clients or complainants. Note: One or two complaints are not uncommon if the person has been in business awhile. Ten or twenty means there is a problem.

Check out Yelp and other crowdsourced review sites
Some service providers will be on Yelp and some may not. There is at least one "tracker" on the West Coast who has over twenty-five very angry complainants. That level of frustrated and unsatisfied customers is too high for this type of work.

Check state-licensing requirements
Most states require a private investigator or detective's license to pursue missing-pet cases. California, Missouri, Florida, Tennessee and Oklahoma are just some of the states that require a license.

For a complete list of states and their licensing requirements, go to this link http://www.howtofindalost-dog.org/additional-references---resources.html.

Stay calm and focused on your search. If the story or offer sounds threatening, fishy, or too complicated, it is best to step away or at least do further research before you move forward.

There are updates and more information at http://www.howtofindalostdog.org/more-about-myths-and-scams.html.

Behavior Basics—
Interaction and Reaction

Is your dog C4T or STARS?

"Dog behavior is the coordinated responses of an individual or groups of dogs to an internal or external stimuli."

LEVITUS, DANIEL ET AL, ANIMAL BEHAVIOR, 2009.03.18

When a dog goes missing, there are many circumstances and situations to take into consideration. First and foremost, it is important to understand the missing dog's basic tendencies toward interactions and reactions. In our work, the first profile we develop is a basic behavioral profile based on these two criteria.

We refer to dogs that are confident in nature as C4T. This acronym briefly describes behaviors a dog may exhibit when interacting with people, other dogs, and the world in general. These canines can be confident, calm, courageous, cooperative, and most of all trusting of humans. In contrast, STARS dogs may be shy, timid, aloof, reserved, or skittish. A STARS dog tends to be reactive and untrusting of strangers. This distinction between C4T and STARS dogs is the first step in developing a strategy to find and recover a missing dog.

Many of the questions on the profiling queries found in each missing-dog scenario will ask you to decide if your dog is C4T or STARS. Ninety percent of our missing-dog cases are canines that exhibit STARS behaviors.

The C4T Behavior Profile: Confident, Calm, Courageous, Cooperative, and Trusting of Humans

Dogs that exhibit this basic behavior profile are generally perceived by people they meet as being friendly and gregarious dogs. They approach new people and situations with gusto. These dogs tend to be calm when exposed to new situations and will readily approach strangers.

Below is a summary of a case we worked for a dog with a C4T profile.

Case Study: Pedro

Pedro went missing from his home on the Fourth of July. The tiny five-pound Chihuahua bolted after fireworks went off nearby. His family began to search for him immediately, but the tiny dog had vanished into the night.

Pedro had been missing ten days when I was initially contacted by his distraught family. After profiling the case, I felt that the tiny dog had been found by a citizen. Pedro is a very outgoing and friendly dog. He exhibited most of the C4T characteristics. Due to his trusting nature and the fact that he had vanished without a trace quickly, I set up a strategy based on a recovery-by-citizen scenario.

Whenever a dog goes missing near a public event that people may be attending from outside the area, it is necessary to expand the search out several miles. During this case, we expanded the focused search area three times. On day twenty-six of Pedro's missing event, we initiated another campaign eleven miles from the point where Pedro had last been seen.

On day twenty-eight, Pedro's family received a call from a man who stated that he thought he may have found tiny Pedro. He explained that he lived forty miles away but he had been at a Fourth of July event near Pedro's home. The gentleman's cousin had recently called and told him that he had just seen several lost-dog signs near the freeway with a picture of the Chihuahua he had found. The caller lived much further away, but his cousin lived near the area where the newest campaign had been initiated. He went on to explain that on the Fourth of July, a tiny Chihuahua had come running up to him. He said he looked around for the owner, but at the end of the event, he had not found the dog's owner, so he had taken him home with him. The finder had not pursued any other avenues to find Pedro's family.

The STARS Behavior Profile

Regardless of the escape event or situation, when a shy, timid, aloof, reserved, or skittish (STARS) dog escapes or goes missing, immediate and decisive action needs to be implemented to recover the frightened dog who is now facing the world alone.

Many STARS dogs will have a combination of the following behaviors and backgrounds:

- The dog may have been adopted from a shelter or rescue.
- The dog may have been found stray or even been born as a feral stray.
- The dog may have begun life in a puppy mill, hoarding situation, or large breeding operation.
- The dog may have been genetically predisposed from birth to shy, skittish behavior.
- The dog may have experienced abuse, neglect, or negative reinforcement in its life.
- The dog may be untrusting of humans or may be slow to warm up to new people.

Dogs with the STARS profile are not as likely to allow a stranger to approach and thus will roam or wander when on their own.

Below is a summary of a case I worked for a dog with STARS tendencies. Please note the pet owner's initial assessment of her dog and how that changed as the case progressed.

Case Study: Sadie

When the pet owner initially called me, the conversation went like this:

Pet owner: My tiny dachshund disappeared. I don't have any sightings, but she loves food, so she probably ran down to the McDonald's on the corner, and when she got there, someone picked her up in a car because she is gorgeous. She has been missing three days, and no one has seen her.

TarQwyn: Have there been any sightings?

Pet owner: No, I really don't think so. One man said he saw her the day after she went missing, but that was almost a mile away, and Sadie would not go that far. There is a busy street near there, and she would never go near a street like that.

TarQwyn: Did you follow up on that sighting?

Pet owner: No, it was too far away, and I think someone at McDonald's must have got her.

During the review of this case, it was clear that the pet owner had preconceived ideas about what had happened to Sadie and what the little dog would and would not do. Initially, she was not open to other possibilities, so when she received other information that did not match what she believed to be true, she discounted the information and did not pursue the leads. This is a classic example of *developing the plot before the evidence comes in*.

Once I pointed out the following, the family was on board to do whatever it took to find the tiny dachshund.

- The pet owner agreed Sadie was a STARS (shy, timid, aloof, reserved, or skittish) dog.
- She also remembered that Sadie would not allow friends and strangers to approach her even in her home.
- I explained that although Sadie might love food, when a dog first escapes she is not focused on food. The owner also remembered that Sadie had just eaten dinner, so she was not hungry at all.
- Upon further investigation, it was discovered that Sadie had experienced a traumatic escape event. Fireworks went off next door, and she bolted in fear. When dogs are in bolting behavior, they run first and think later. A dog running from fireworks, gunshots, or thunder can travel huge distances. A mile away after sixteen hours being gone was not very far for a healthy, young dachshund.

What really happened to Sadie:

Upon taking this case, we immediately put together an expansive community-awareness campaign. Initially the pet owner thought we were going out too far, but she humored us and did as we asked.

Our strategy spanned five miles in each direction while using the river that was just east of Sadie's point of escape as a boundary and probable travel route. In addition, we did a custom phone alert with Lost My Doggie alerting the local residents in the rural, wooded area that the tiny dachshund might be wandering near their home.

We also had the pet owner take a photo identification lineup card to the witness who thought he had seen Sadie the day after she went missing. He did pick Sadie out of the lineup. It is most likely that he did in fact see her, as the dachshund's eventual direction of travel was in the direction of the man's house.

On day six, the call came in from a man who lived along the river—five miles away. He said he had seen a tiny dachshund run into the woods near where the river forked. Sadie's whole family loaded up and went to the fork of the river. They each began to walk in the woods, quietly calling out Sadie's pet names. Within thirty minutes, the pet owner turned around to find Sadie following her. It took another ten minutes for her to come to her family, but she was recovered, and a reunion was celebrated.

Note: It is likely Sadie would have traveled further up the river had she hit the fork in the river, which would have caused her to have to travel inland as she could not get around the fork. Her family was surprised she had made it five miles away and that she had crossed several busy streets during her journey. It is highly likely that she would have traveled much further had it not been for the topography and fork in the river.

The Nine Scenarios
Profiling , Analysis and Strategies

Introduction To The Nine Scenarios

When a dog goes missing..

Anytime someone or something is missing, a deduction of what happened and where it happened must be decided upon. Information is gathered and a decision is made as to how to proceed to find the subject, object or person. This process is done through assessment of the situation and a profile of the subject and environment. This process is most commonly used in the search for a missing person. Just as in a missing person case, the search and investigation for a missing dog is also based on these factors.

There are nine scenarios under which a dog can go missing. Profiling a missing dog case to arrive at the most likely scenario includes identifying the behavioral characteristics of the lost dog and comparing that information to the missing event, location and terrain to arrive at the most likely scenario the subject dog is experiencing.

Each missing dog situation must be analyzed on an individual basis. When a dog goes missing, an educated, consistent and effective strategy based on the most likely scenario should be employed as quickly as possible.

In the following section, each of the nine scenarios will be presented along with a query form and characteristics that may be present with each. Each scenario will also include a list of suggested techniques to implement in your recovery strategy.

The Dog That Is Found by a Citizen

The dog that experiences a recovery by a citizen is off its property. The dog may be on a public street or in a public area, or it may be on the private property of another. The dog has been discovered by a citizen who decides to recover the animal for safety and return it or sometimes for other less altruistic reasons.

Profiling Query for a Dog That Has Been Found by a Citizen

Determining factors: Below are some of the questions to consider when profiling for this scenario.

1. Is your dog gregarious and outgoing?
2. Does your dog exhibit the C4T behavior profile (confident, calm, courageous, cooperative, and trusting of humans)?
3. In his normal everyday life, does your dog run up to strangers?
4. If your dog has escaped before, has someone else ever returned or found the dog?
5. Has anyone reported seeing your dog in the company of a stranger?
6. Has your dog ever been picked up by animal control or other government entity?
7. Does your dog like to ride in vehicles?
8. Could your dog be considered a unique, gorgeous, or a highly desirable breed?
9. Have there been any leads wherein the dog was seen getting into a vehicle?

The Situations When a Dog Is Found by a Citizen

There are five situations that can happen when a dog is found by a citizen.

The majority of citizen recoveries are *Samaritan Rescues*, with the rescuer's intent being to find the animal's rightful owner. This is the most common situation and what we all hope for when a dog goes missing. Unfortunately, if the dog does not have on identification in the form of an easy-to-use phone number, the extent that individuals will go to find a dog's owner varies depending on the individual's ethics, background, and task-management skills. Dogs with only a veterinary or rabies tag are not in a much better situation than a dog without ID, as many people will not take the time to do the research to find the owner. When children find a dog, they may call the phone number on a tag or collar, but they generally will not call the "dog pound" or a Vet's office from the tags.

In some circumstances, a Samaritan rescue can result in a *Finders Keepers* or *Rescuer Re-home* situation. The most likely dogs to experience either of these situations are those that do not have the pet owner's current phone number on a tag or their collar. Most people's natural and compulsive tendency is to call the number on the tag or collar. It is when the pet has been with its rescuer or finder for a period of time that the citizen may decide to keep the pet or rehome it on his or her own. Small toy dogs, fluffy or white dogs, and unique dogs of a desirable breed are more likely than other breeds or crosses to experience these situations.

In other circumstances, certain dogs may be *Recovered for Reward* and retained with the individual's intent being to collect the reward. This most often happens with dogs the finder feels are cherished family members or an "expensive breed." *Seized for Resale* is a situation where the dog is seized from the street with the intent being to sell the dog. English bulldogs, French bulldogs, Pugs, Yorkshire terriers, and any other dog that a finder presumes is valuable can experience this situation.

The following represent the criteria that are the most likely to exist in the found-by-citizen scenario.

Profile
The most likely pet to experience this scenario is a friendly, outgoing individual, sometimes referred to as a people lover. The list includes also many of the following:

- Tiny and small breeds such as the Yorkshire terrier, Pomeranian, Chihuahua, and other dogs that are considered desirable, including small dogs that are mixes and are in this size range.
- White pets and fluffy or long-haired pets.
- Puppies or older dogs that appear to be puppies.
- Purebred dogs.
- Exotic or unique dogs like the Afghan hound, Old English sheepdog, and all the varieties of bulldogs.
- Small dogs that freeze in fear when someone attempts to approach or pick them up.
- A pet that has been injured, especially if the rescuer perceives the injury as a sign of abuse or neglect.
- Shy, timid, aloof, reserved, or skittish dogs *are not as likely* to allow recovery by a citizen unless they freeze or roll over on their back when approached.

Characteristics, Sightings, and Leads
The following are the most likely situations experienced in this scenario as the search and time go on.

- Will have fewer sightings than other situations; possibly even none depending on when the pet was rescued.
- Bystanders or witnesses may have seen a car stop or slow down near point last seen.
- The pet was last seen in a public place like a park, the middle of a street or busy intersection, or a public pool, with no further sightings.

- The pet was last seen playing with children that the pet owner might or might not know.
- Witnesses reported the dog running up to people while out roaming.

Case Study: Lola
Samaritan Recovery or Rescue

Hanging out with her family while they were working in the yard, Lola, a four-month-old Chihuahua cross, went missing when her owner turned his back to turn off the hose.

Lola's family searched the area for hours. Their little dog appeared to have just disappeared. She had been missing forty-eight hours when her family called for help. The puppy and missing event profiled as a likely "found by citizen" scenario, so a public-awareness campaign was designed, and the pet owners sprang into action to fulfil the required tasks on the strategy.

Twelve hours later, the call came in. Lola had run to a park twelve blocks away where a senior citizen noticed the obviously lost puppy. Not wanting to leave the young puppy in the big park, she took her home with her. Lola had only been missing for forty-five minutes when the kindly woman found her. Three days later, when she went to the grocery store, the finder saw the campaign in effect and called the distraught family.

Lola was returned within the hour.

Case Study: Willie and Miracle
Finders Keepers and Rescuer Re-home

Willie and his sister had been exhibiting bored and anxious behavior for a few weeks before deciding to jump the fence and go on the roam. They had been missing almost two weeks when our team was called in. The tracking dogs tracked Willie to a house where the resident had found Willie's sister, Miracle, but the citizen denied having the big black male Great Dane. Miracle was recovered.

The tracking dogs were started again from a sighting a mile and a half away. Cade and two other tracking dogs tracked back to the woman's house and then confirmed Willie's scent at the house. We knew that the resident was not telling the truth and had at one time had Willie on her property just as she had Miracle. The citizen became aggressive and threatening as we tried to unravel the story, so we decided to leave the area. Willie was found the next day by a girl who said the big dog had been in a neighbor's yard but was suddenly "turned loose." Having seen the campaign in effect in her neighborhood, she called the number on the sign as soon she saw the huge Great Dane walking down the street.

Our investigation uncovered that Willie had in fact been picked up by the woman and kept at her house. Willie was either sold or rehomed to a man on the street where he was found. The tracking dogs' undisputed belief that Willie had been at the house led to this recovery. Neighbors explained that the captor's house had been used as a meth lab, and the residents "did not want the law around." The captor became alarmed that we would bring the police with us when we returned to continue our search and more than likely alerted Willie's captor, who turned him loose.

Case Study: Hunter and Robin
Seized for Resale

Hunter and Robin had been missing nine weeks when we arrived on scene to begin the investigation. Doggie mom Pat, a retired senior citizen, was an emotional wreck after spending most of the past two months tirelessly searching for the two dogs.

Hunter and Robin had escaped their yard one morning when Pat went for coffee and grocery shopping. When she arrived back home, her gate was ajar, and the two French bulldogs were gone. A frantic search began.

Lead dog Cade quickly found Hunter's scent and headed down the driveway and across the street to a business adjacent to Pat's property. As we were tracking in the parking lot, a young man came out and reported that he thought he knew what had happened to the dogs.

Angry at his employer, he told us that the business owner's grandson had found the dogs and sold them to a woman who he thought had sold the dogs to someone else in a town twenty-five miles away, but he did not know who the person was or where the dogs were.

We moved our investigation to the tiny rural town twenty-five miles away. By using the dog team and investigator know-how, we were able to find the dogs and get the sheriff to confiscate them.

We learned that the dogs had been sold before Pat even knew they had escaped the yard. No one was ever held responsible or prosecuted.

Case Study: Priscilla

Held for Reward

Priscilla was found and held for reward. Positive negotiations and a cool head brought her home.

It was a day filled with joy and celebration as well as sadness and disappointment when Priscilla, a thirteen-month-old Yorkshire terrier, came home. Happiness because she was home safe and sound; sadness because of the steps necessary to recover her.

Headed for a new start in the New Year, Priscilla and her owner, Tracey, had just moved to a new state. On their second day in their new hometown, Priscilla got out the front door without anyone realizing it. When discovered, the family quickly spread out scouring the neighborhood in search of the small five-pound dog. At the end of day one, no one had seen the tiny canine.

On day three a panicked Tracey called me. They had discovered that someone had seen Priscilla on the day she went missing. She was being chased by a woman who was trying to catch her; Priscilla had not been seen since. The family was devastated, as they realized that whoever had their family member had to know they were looking for her. The apartment complex where she had been seen was covered with posters and fliers pleading for information about their much-loved dog. Whoever had Priscilla knew her heartbroken family was searching for her.

I assured Tracey that by working quickly, a plan could be developed to encourage the finder to return her. Within hours the plan was in effect, and by day's end, the expected call came in. The man on the phone said he had the small dog but wanted to know what the reward was. I had coached the family on their responses and protocol to follow. After a few minutes of negotiation on the reward, the man agreed, and the transfer of money and dog were negotiated. Priscilla was home within the hour.

Actions and Activities to Pursue

You need to keep an open mind and be patient while waiting for the finder or someone who has information about your dog to call you. The recovery plan for this scenario is about awareness. The more people who know your dog is missing, the quicker will be the recovery. Your goal is to alert 25 percent of the community every day that your dog is missing and that you are working to find him.

Below is a checklist of the techniques and activities to pursue if you believe your dog is experiencing this scenario and one of these situations. The techniques and actions suggested are described in detail in **Section 3: Actions, Activities, and Techniques.**

In the first forty-eight hours, do the following:

- Follow the **first-response protocol** found in Section 3, to ascertain your dog is off your property.
- Perform a **ground-zero search** of your home or the point of escape, unless a sighting has been confirmed outside of ground zero.
- Get **signs** up ASAP. Use one of the suggested formats and get them done. Our preference is the eleven-by-seventeen laminated signs done by Staples, Office Depot, or Office Max. They are quick to set up and ready to hang within a day.
- **Check emergency animal hospitals by phone** as this is the most expedient way to inquire of these facilities and leave your missing pet's description and your phone number.
- **Check animal shelters**, animal control, humane societies, and other locations where stray dogs are held. This is a required activity and it must be done regularly. Please go to the shelter in person as opposed to just checking online and by phone.
- **If the dog is a purebred or looks like a purebred**, call the breed rescue to see if a citizen has turned a dog in recently and, if possible elicit their assistance. Many cities now boast a rescue for everything, which is great on one hand and time-consuming on the other. Check any rescue where your dog could possibly end up.

Developing the strategy

Unless you absolutely know someone has rescued your dog, you must cover all the bases until one scenario is absolutely established. Fortunately, many of the scenarios overlap in technique and action.

- Keep a **sightings journal**. I recommend that you respond to sightings immediately. When a dog has been rescued, there may not be any sightings, as the dog could have been picked up very quickly. In other cases, neighbors, drivers passing by, and even relatives of the rescuers may give information that leads to the return of the dog.
- **Develop witnesses** as you would for any other scenario near the point of escape for sightings, information, and leads. If you receive a sightings call or someone states that their neighbor, acquaintance, and so on has a new dog that looks like yours, you need to proceed cautiously.

Sometimes it's a knock on the door and the rescuer hands you your dog; sometimes it can be more difficult. Above all, do not accuse or become aggressive.

- Use a **neighborhood grid search** when developing witnesses.
- Create a **photo identification lineup** card to help confirm that the dog the witnesses have seen is in fact your dog.

Community-awareness campaign

Pursue a **community-awareness campaign**. In almost every scenario, this is important. Think about when there is a missing person, Law Enforcement relies on the community to bring forth clues and leads. It is the same with a missing dog.

- Use the community-awareness **signs** I recommend for sightings at the point of escape and near confirmed sightings.
- Proceed to **flyers** as calling cards.
- Place an **ad in the newspaper**. See the instructions for writing an ad for a dog found by citizen.
- **Post** on lost-and-found websites, on social media sites and on missing-pet alert groups. The ads and postings should include locations last seen.
- **Post** your missing dog to your Facebook profile, and encourage others to share the post. A Facebook page specific to your missing dog can increase awareness. Instagram and other social media platforms can also be helpful.
- **Media involvement** is very tough in this scenario unless there is something special about your dog or you. Think and then angle your story accordingly.
- **Hire a professional** with scent-specific tracking dogs specially trained to follow the scent of missing dogs. A properly trained scent-specific dog can alert you if your dog has been picked up in a vehicle and most importantly where she was picked up. Once this location is established, you can refine your strategy and awareness campaign incorporating this data.

There are additional instructions and suggestions at http://www.howtofindalostdog.org/more-about-the-nine-scenarios.html.

The Roaming Dog

This dog has gone missing and is living or wandering at large. It includes all dogs that remain at large and are not able to find their way home.

Profiling Query for a Dog That Is Roaming at Large
Determining factors: Below are some of the factors to consider for this scenario.

1. Does your dog have any of the STARS behaviors (shy, timid, aloof, reserved, or skittish)?
2. Does the dog shy away from strangers or act reticent when a stranger attempts to approach?
3. Is the dog missing in an area that he is unfamiliar with?
4. Does this dog bolt, run, or hide when frightened?
5. Has this dog escaped before?
6. If your dog has escaped before, have you always had to recover the dog yourself, (he would not let anyone else approach)?
7. Was the dog's missing event caused by a tragic or traumatic escape event?
8. Is the dog one of the more common breeds that tend to roam when lost?
   - Dogs that tend to roam include German Shepherd cross, German Shepherd, Border Collie, Australian Shepherd, Beagle, Bloodhound, Shih Tzu, Yorkshire terrier, Pomeranian, Dachshund, Chihuahua, Greyhound, Whippet, Italian Greyhound, Siberian husky, Miniature Pinscher, Havanese, Shiba Inu, Brittany Spaniel, and other hunting dogs and hounds as well as any dog crossed with any of these breeds.
9. Has there been more than one sighting of the dog since he went missing?
10. Is your dog a rescue that may have been stray or feral at some time is his life?

The Roaming Dog at Large Scenario
Most pets in this category are dogs that exhibit a STARS behavior profile, (dogs that may be shy, timid, aloof, reserved, or skittish). Dogs that are displaced or have become lost in an area outside of their home territory are also candidates for this scenario. This can include dogs that recently moved

to the area and are unfamiliar with it, were on vacation with their owners, or were being taken care of by a caregiver either at their home or away from their home. Regardless of the circumstances, the dog is now at large and alone in a place that he is unfamiliar with. In addition, some pets are escape artists and try to get out all the time because it is fun and exciting. These Houdinis may wander aimlessly, not realizing they have traveled well beyond their known home territory and are now lost.

Profile

Following are the indicators for a dog that may be roaming:

- The most common indicator is the dog has a STARS (shy, timid, aloof, reserved, or skittish) behavior profile. Dogs that exhibit any of the STARS characteristics, or are reactive, are the most likely dogs to pursue this scenario. Many of these dogs lack trust toward humans.
- A dog that is displaced for one reason or another. This pet may have been on vacation with the owner, being boarded at a kennel, groomer, or veterinarian's office; staying with someone other than the pet owner; recently moved to a new home; or in a myriad of situations that result in the dog being in a place that is not its known home territory. The dog does not have a bonded interest in the location, which causes it to wander and ultimately learn to adapt to survive on its own.
- Dogs in the herding, hound, and sporting groups are the most likely to wander. Other breeds that more commonly choose to wander are the Jack Russell terrier, Beagle, Shih Tzu, Yorkie, Whippet, Greyhound, and herding group crosses. Any dog can choose to wander, but some breeds are more susceptible to it—probably because they tend to be more successful at it.
- Dogs that may have been feral or were captured as strays when they were younger may also revert to wandering when presented with an unknown situation regardless how young they were when domesticated.
- Males, both neutered and unaltered, seem more likely to stay at large and not seek human help, as opposed to females. However, a female at large may travel further than a male in the same situation.
- Environments with an open space, wooded area, farmlands, or greenbelt access with creeks or drainage ditches seem to encourage this behavior.
- Dogs that don't fit this profile can become roaming dogs if they are released after being stolen, rescued, or displaced.

Typical Sightings Pattern

The pattern of sightings with this scenario will vary depending on the dog, the escape event, and the environment.

- As a rule of thumb, citizens may initially respond with sightings of the dog in various areas. After two or three days, these sightings may decrease and in some cases will cease all together. The decrease is usually due to the dog traveling outside of the owner's search area, the area that the owner has primarily focused on since the pet has been missing.

- Experience has proven that most pet owners keep their search confined to areas they feel the dog will frequent. They may avoid situations they feel their dog would not approach, like a busy street or freeway. Most of the time when the sightings stop, the pet has traveled outside the search area and has crossed into areas or situations that the pet owner feels are out of character for the pet. I frequently remind panicked pet owners that their dog is in an unusual situation that he may not have faced before. Most pet owners do not know how their dog responds or the behaviors he exhibits when they are not around.

- I generally recommend that pet owners expand their search area to include those areas, streets, and situations that they feel their pet would not pursue. The expansion of the search area usually increases the sightings of the wandering dog at least in the first week or so. If fortunate, the dog will settle into a routine and territory quickly, which will then allow citizens and witnesses the opportunity to see him more than once.

- However, not all dogs settle into a territory and routine. Some breeds like terriers, beagles, Shiba Inus, huskies, and sight hounds may continue to wander nomadically. Dogs exhibiting nomadic behavior are among the toughest to locate and capture, as many times their needs are being met while on the roam. In my experience, dogs in the herding group are the most likely to settle into an area, with many doing so in the second or third week.

- Some dogs will begin to establish a pattern and routine to fulfill their needs for security, water, food, and shelter. By far the most important of these is water, and if the surrounding area does not offer water resources, dogs in these areas will generally stay close to a lake, creek, or other water source. Dogs in areas abundant with water may choose food as their most important resource and may stick closer to the area and situation they have found will supply food on a regular basis. Dumpsters, garbage cans, and restaurant alleys are all popular feeding stations for the dog on the run. People who routinely feed cats on their front porch or in a public-access area may observe the food disappearing at a faster rate than normal if a dog is roaming nearby.

- The least important of the big three necessities is shelter, and in only a very limited number of cases have I known a dog to stay in one area because of shelter. The exception to this is when it is storming, snowing, or extremely cold. These conditions can cause a dog to stay in a warmer sheltered area, but not always.

- Sightings may happen in the early morning and evenings and less often during the day. Most dogs in this situation return to a more feral survival pattern and forage for food and water at night or near dawn when fewer people are around. Witnesses may report that the dog appeared to be trotting along as if on a mission. Sometimes they are seen drinking or eating. Many times a witness will remark that the dog looked like he was having a good time. I think this is an accurate statement for many pets. Some dogs begin to enjoy the wandering lifestyle, and many do not even lose weight during their journey.

- Many displaced dogs, lost in an area that is not their home territory, may continue to travel farther and farther away from the point of escape, leading some pet owners to believe that the dog will eventually find its way home. In my experience this is relatively rare; Lassie always makes it home without help, but most displaced dogs do not.

Case Study: Mishka

Mishka, a Border collie mix, was lost from a dog-boarding facility where she was staying while her owner was traveling out of town for the Thanksgiving holiday. Mishka, an energetic black dog of medium size, was a good jumper and suffered with separation anxiety when her owner was away. The shy dog was dropped off at the boarding facility the Wednesday morning before Thanksgiving Day. She was lost by four o'clock the same day after jumping two interior barriers and escaping out the front door of the lobby.

During the search for Mishka, we found that we were getting sightings and leads from four other black dogs all lost and roaming in the same area. The K9 Team worked diligently to discover which sightings were Mishka and which were not. Mishka traveled a four-mile area, frequently returning to the area near to where she had gone missing. In all Mishka was on the roam for ten days.

During that time we were able to get newscast coverage that highlighted the search area and that Mishka was still missing. Even though Mishka was hit by a car on day one of her escape event, she thrived and survived during her journey.

On day ten, a sighting came in behind a car dealership, and it was Mishka. Her family was only minutes away from the location. They raced to dealership and saw Mishka slinking back toward the woods. Within seconds of hearing her mom's quiet and calm voice, Mishka ran straight into her open arms.

Perhaps one of the more unique characteristics of this case is that Mishka was not food motivated throughout this ordeal. Her focus was her owner. Once she was near enough to Lauren to identify her, she quickly responded and ran to her. Although Lassie did this every night on television, many roaming dogs do not.

Additional roaming-dog stories and case studies can be found on the website at http://www.howtofindalostdog.org/roaming-dog-recovery-stories.html.

Locating the Roaming Dog: Getting to the Same Place at the Same Time

Most people are sure their pampered hound could not possibly survive the night without sleeping on their bed. In fact, in almost every case, this is just not true. From the overweight couch-potato Cocker spaniel to the arthritic fourteen-year-old Golden Retriever to the tiny five-pound Yorkshire terrier who only eats salmon at home, all have ended up roaming and survived. In many cases these dogs have thrived without even losing a pound.

Locating and recovering a roaming dog is a process, and it is best if you approach this endeavor in this way, or you will become discouraged and frustrated.

The typical steps are as follows:

1. You will create awareness of your missing dog's situation and ask for help from the public.
2. You will keep a consistent public-awareness campaign in front of the community where the dog is roaming.
3. You will respond to calls and sightings immediately (the "go sees"), using techniques to discover if the dog the witness saw is in fact your dog.
4. Ultimately we are looking for one of two calls.
   - I am looking at your dog now—you need to rush and get to the location while keeping the caller on the phone.
   - I saw your dog today or last night, or I have seen this dog more than once in this area.
5. When a sighting or lead is confirmed as your dog, you will move your search parameters and create awareness in the new area.

If Your Dog Is Roaming: Your Feelings

Feelings of sadness and grief are common in any missing-pet situation, but the emotions in this scenario can surprise some people. Many grief-stricken pet owners express feelings of betrayal and anger toward their wandering dog. In their eyes, their dog has made a choice and is choosing to stay out on the road instead of coming home. In the case of the shy dog, many do not understand how the dog that shares their bed is now acting as if she does not know them. Others express feelings of shock when they have seen their dog on the street and then called knowing their loving pet would gratefully run to them. They are shocked and then hurt when the dog bolts and runs away. These are very common human feelings for very expected canine behaviors in this situation.

The most important thing to remember is that your much-loved pet is a dog, not a human. I always caution people experiencing an at-large dog to expect her to run from them and prepare emotionally for that outcome. They should be grateful and surprised if the opposite occurs. A dog's feelings of love are felt by her in a way that we cannot understand, because we are not of her species. Her natural instincts are not our natural instincts. At her core, no matter the relationship she has with you, she is still a canine with a genetic makeup more similar to that of the wolf and coyote than ours.

If your dog is wandering like her feral cousins, my best course of advice is to be emotionally prepared and to not take any of the dog's behaviors personally. Her love for you is expressed in many ways, but she is not human, and this is not the time to put human personality traits and characteristics on her. Think like a wolf or coyote, which will more closely model her tendencies on this journey.

Actions and Activities to Pursue

You need diligence and patience in this pursuit. I find that the roaming dog can be the most difficult case to pursue. This is not because of the mechanics of the search or the activities but due to the extreme amount of patience that is required on your part. No one act is going to bring this dog home; instead, it will be a succession of tasks and a consistent effort that ultimately will lead to reunion. You must be patient and diligent.

Below is a checklist of the techniques and activities you should pursue if you believe your dog is in this situation. The techniques and actions suggested are described in detail in **Section 3: Actions, Activities, and Techniques.**

In the beginning

- Follow the **first-response protocol** for the first forty-eight hours. Even if your dog has been missing more than forty-eight hours, it is wise to scan this section. Pay particular attention to the instructions on approaching or in most cases not approaching the roaming dog.
- Perform a **ground-zero search** of your home or the point of escape, unless a sighting has been confirmed outside your property.

Developing the strategy

- Keep a **sightings journal**. I recommend that you respond to sightings immediately. Don't be surprised if your dog does not respond to your calls as she usually does. It is very common for even a friendly and bold dog to revert to a survival mind-set and temporarily abandon her domestic training.
- Please read "How to Approach or, More Precisely, *Not* Approach the Roaming Dog." Even if you are absolutely sure your dog will sprint into your arms, please humor me and read this. After forty-eight hours, it is so common for the dog to not approach and to run off that it is considered to be the norm in our work. Read this even if you know you will not need it.
- **Develop witnesses** as you would for any other scenario near the point of escape for sightings, information, and leads.
- Create a **photo identification lineup** card to help confirm that the dog the witnesses see is in fact your dog. This is critical tool for the roaming-dog scenario, as we need to determine if sightings are confirmed before redefining our strategy based on the new sightings.
- **Hire a professional** with scent-specific tracking dogs specially trained to follow the scent of missing dogs. The roaming dog is one of the most difficult to recover, and therefore, a professional is particularly warranted. An investigator with K9s can locate the wanderer so that attraction techniques and capture can begin. Be sure you hire a professional with at least fifty

missing-dog cases under his or her belt and a record of successes. Read this section and do the tasks suggested before hiring anyone, or you may find you have wasted your money.

- **Check emergency animal hospitals by phone**, as this is the most expedient way to inquire of these facilities and leave your missing pet's description and your phone number.
- **Check animal shelters**, humane societies, and so on. Roaming dogs can be perceived as a nuisance, and animal control may be called by a resident to catch the pet that has been hanging around. Remember to inquire and view animals in the veterinary or "injured animal" area.

Community-awareness campaign

- Set up or purchase **community-awareness signs**. Place signs for sightings at the point of escape and near confirmed sightings.
- Proceed to **flyers** as calling cards. Flyers should state that you need the community to help in discovering the pet's routine to help him get home. Normally I advise against using the pet's name on flyers, but in the roaming-dog case, a phrase such as "Help Ringo get home" can greatly increase the public involvement. One pet owner added, "He's a traveling man and we are trying to help him find home" to bring some whimsy to the situation in hopes that people would remember their missing dog if in fact they did see him.
- Consider placing **car signs** on all vehicles involved in the search for your dog. This is the scenario where the car signs can be the most effective.
- **Post** on lost-and-found websites and missing-pet alert groups. The ads and postings should include locations where the dog was last seen.
- If your dog is roaming, **social media** can be one of the quickest ways to get his situation out to the masses. Post your missing dog to your Facebook profile and encourage others to share the post. If your dog is gone longer than forty-eight hours, a Facebook page can be helpful. Instagram and other social media platforms can be helpful also.
- The good news about the roaming dog is that the **media** may be interested in the search, and they can be genuinely helpful. The media can provide continuing coverage for dogs at large for months; the continuing saga of each dog makes an appealing story.

Attraction, surveillance, and capture

- Use a **magnet or lure animal** or pet to attract the wanderer. This is one of the most successful techniques in attracting and ultimately capturing a dog at large.
- Create a **feeding-and-comfort station**. Once territory or routine sightings are established, many of these dogs must be lured in or attracted to allow capture.
- **Surveillance and monitoring** of areas where sightings are concentrated may be needed.

- **Humane trapping:** Dogs that have reverted to feral habits often won't come to their owners. Humane traps built for the capture of dogs can be necessary.
- **The enclosure trap:** Many dogs will not go into a humane box trap. An enclosure trap may be necessary.

There are additional instructions and suggestions at http://www.howtofindalostdog.org/more-about-the-nine-scenarios.html.

The Stolen Dog

Although many people believe their dog has been stolen when they call for help, this scenario is rarely the case. That said, the instances of stolen dogs and the reasons they are stolen have increased over the past decade.

Profiling Query for a Dog That Has Been Stolen

Below are some of the questions to consider for this scenario.

1. Is your dog gone without a trace? No sightings or leads?
2. Will your dog allow a stranger to approach? If not, are there people your dog will allow to approach?
3. Is your dog one of the breeds that are considered valuable or desirable?
   - These breeds have a higher incidence of theft than other breeds: Yorkshire terrier, English bulldog, French bulldog, Afghan hound, Pug, small fluffy designer dogs, hunting dogs, Cane Corso, pit bull (particularly those dogs that are gray, blue, or black in color), and dogs that are unique in appearance or rare in breed.
4. Has anyone reported any suspicious people or activities in the area in the past six months (e.g., car driving slowly, man or woman taking pictures on the street)?
5. Did the dog go missing in a rural area?
6. Are there other dogs missing in the area?
7. Have witnesses reported a suspicious vehicle in the area?
8. Are there people in your life who may want to cause you distress?
9. Is there anyone who has shown a particular interest in your dog?
10. Was your dog tied out or behind a chain-link fence when he went missing?
11. Were there any visible clues left by the thieves that would cause a prudent person to believe the dog was stolen? Example: the dog is missing after a burglary or a lock was cut.

There are three reasons why a dog might be stolen:

- For resale—if it is a desirable breed or is unique in some way
- An individual has an interest in the pet for any reason, including affection and a working purpose
- As revenge to hurt or cause the pet owner distress

What constitutes a stolen dog?

For a pet to be considered stolen, it must be removed bodily from its own property or property that belongs to its owner or acting guardian in much the same way that a stereo or car is stolen.

A dog outside its property is legally considered stray, and the laws protecting the pet owner in the case of someone rescuing the animal from a public place or on the property of another vary from state to state. So be careful with this definition when talking to law enforcement. If someone has picked up your dog on the street, even if they know this is your dog, legally they have picked up a stray, and the law is very gray on the protocol for this from state to state and city to city.

In some states the police will become actively involved in a true stolen-pet case, while in other locations the local law enforcement may feel possession is nine-tenths of the law. My best advice is if you feel your pet was actually stolen and there is evidence to support it, call the police immediately and gently but persuasively encourage their involvement. Do not threaten or in any way become misaligned with the investigating officer, regardless of whether it seems he or she is not taking your case seriously. Better to keep the officer on your side and be helpful with your input rather than pushy and threatening.

My suggestion in a true stolen-pet case: hire a private investigator licensed in your area who is familiar with recovering stolen property, which unfortunately is what a dog is considered in most states.

Profile

Any pet can be the victim of theft. Some environmental situations and dog breeds are more likely than others to experience this situation. The following meet the profile.

- Skittish, xenophobic, and aggressive pets are *less likely* to be stolen.
- Outgoing, unique, cute, and exotic pets or pets presumed to be expensive or valuable in some way are more likely to be stolen.
- Pets that are kept in an area clearly visible from the public streets or public areas are more at risk.
- Dogs that are tied out in the open, surrounded by a radio fence, or behind a chain-link fence are more susceptible to theft than dogs behind a privacy fence.
- Dogs that live on a corner lot have a higher risk of theft due to the visibility from the front and side yards.
- Certain breeds appear to be stolen more frequently. Examples: Yorkshire terrier, English bulldog, French bulldog, Afghan hound, pug, small fluffy designer dogs, hunting dogs, Cane Corso.

- In some areas the pit bull is also coveted and stolen frequently. The most common pit to be stolen is gray/blue and white followed by black and white. Males and females are equal in desirability, but a spayed female is the least desirable to a thief.
- Areas where there is an active drug trade are more likely to have stolen-pet cases than other areas of similar demographics and income, but stolen-dog cases are on the rise in all areas and demographics.
- There has been an increase in stolen dogs in rural areas over the past five years.

Characteristics, Sightings, and Leads

- No visible means for the pet to have escaped on its own or explanation as to how the dog is now missing. Example: the dog is removed from its kennel, and the security clip is found clipped to the fence.
- There is evidence that would lead a prudent person to believe that the pet has been stolen.
- Pet owner is aware of grievance harbored by another and is concerned *that person has the capacity* to steal his or her pet.
- Pet owner is concerned about someone's feeling of revenge for one reason or another.
- Witness noticed suspicious activities or out-of-the-ordinary behavior in the area the pet was last seen. Example: unfamiliar vehicle in the area near the pet owner's house with no explanation.
- Other pet owners in the area have experienced a similar situation, and their dogs are missing.
- Theft or burglary has occurred at the location, and other items are missing.
- In the case of revenge, an obvious clue is left for the pet owner to see. For example, the dog's collar is removed and left in obvious sight. We have had collars left on front porches and clasped to the fence.
- There are no sightings.

Note: It is common for a stolen pet to end up stray within days or weeks of being stolen, so be diligent in your shelter checks and continued community awareness. Many times a pet is stolen in a spontaneous action, and then the thief is unable to accommodate the animal, so he or she turns the pet loose. That is why it is common for some of these pets to end up as a roaming dog at large. You should read about the roaming dog for activities and tasks that relate to this scenario.

Case Study: Roscoe
Stolen Dog
I received a very panicky call one night. It was 11:30 p.m., and I have learned that these calls are usually emergencies, so I generally take them. Most likely a dog just went missing or has been hit by a car and they can't find her or, as in Roscoe's case, has just been stolen.

When Roscoe's family first entered their yard after returning from work, they knew immediately something was terribly wrong. In their fenced backyard, they found their little beagle's tether line carefully coiled and placed in the middle of their yard. Roscoe was nowhere to be seen. Right away the family knew someone had stolen Roscoe, as he could not have gotten off his long tether, which had been employed as a temporary fix since the little Houdini now made a practice of digging under the fence while everyone was away at work and school. A quick search of the yard and Roscoe's collar with tags was found fastened carefully to the gate where anyone could see it. Roscoe clearly could not have attached his collar to the gate; the friendly little beagle had been abducted, and whoever had taken him wanted to make it clear that Roscoe had been stolen.

A quick sweep of the neighborhood revealed no clues, leads, or sightings. Roscoe had vanished.

After reviewing the case, I queried all the family members to see if they knew of anyone who was angry and had the capacity to plan and carry out this type of crime. At first everyone said no, but the next day, Mary called me. She said they had not considered this at first but now realized that earlier in the week, a strange call had come from one of her husband's past students. They felt this might be a clue.

Three days before Roscoe's abduction, John, a teacher, had received a call from a former student, Jerry. The young man had left high school five years earlier and had since led a troubled life. His call to his former teacher was to tell him that he had ruined his life and that he held him responsible for all the bad things that had transpired since the young man had left school. The call was very troubling to the high-school teacher, and he felt bad for Jerry but did not really see how he had been responsible for the boy's wayward path, and he told him so. Jerry became angry and said he would get back at his former teacher and hung up. John now felt that this call probably had something to do with Roscoe's disappearance.

I told John and Mary to call the police and file a police report explaining the call, the threats, and what had transpired. They were very fortunate, as the officer who came out to take the report was a dog lover and took the case seriously. This officer would be the catalyst for Roscoe's recovery. After taking the report, the officer did a criminal background check on Jerry and found that he was on probation and living with his parents. He contacted Jerry through his parents to notify him of the dog's abduction. Jerry claimed he knew nothing about "any dog theft." The officer told Jerry he would be contacting his probation officer and let him know about Jerry's call to the teacher and what had later transpired with Roscoe. He hung up and immediately called John and Mary to tell them of Jerry's denial of any participation in the abduction.

John and Mary called me to go over what they should do. Their children were devastated, and they felt they could not allow Jerry to get away with this. I agreed to come with my dog team to Wisconsin to find out if Roscoe had been taken by Jerry. I prepared to leave but felt there was a tactic we have used many times in my business that might work. I asked John to call Jerry's parents.

John called Jerry's parents and told them about the crazy and accusatory call he had received from their son. John went on to explain what had happened to their much-loved beagle three days after the call. Jerry's parents assured John that their son would not have taken their dog, because Jerry loved animals. John then let the parents know that he had hired a private investigator to get to the bottom of it all. He told Jerry's parents that the investigator was bringing specially trained tracking dogs that would be able to tell where Roscoe had gone and if he had ever been in Jerry's car or on their property.

Twelve hours later, Roscoe was found twenty-five miles away from his home wandering on a street. He was less than a block from the manufacturing facility where Jerry's father worked. It was clear to all that Jerry had in fact taken the dog and kept him. His parents most likely did not know the dog he brought home belonged to his former teacher until they received the call from the police officer. John's call right after that had frightened them, as he let them know that the tracking dogs would go right to their house if Roscoe was there. Not wanting their son to go back to jail, Jerry's father took Roscoe to work with him and turned him loose. Roscoe was found within fifteen minutes of the beginning of Jerry's father's shift.

No one was ever charged, and the case was closed after Roscoe's recovery.

Actions and Activities to Pursue

Unless you know for sure that your dog was stolen, you need to pursue a basic protocol and cover the most common scenarios indicated for your dog based on his behavior profile. If you know your dog was stolen, proceed as below.

Below is a checklist of the techniques and activities you should pursue if you believe your dog is in this situation. The techniques and actions suggested are described in detail in **Section 3: Actions, Activities, and Techniques.**

If you believe your dog was stolen:
> **Immediately call the police and file a police report.**

- You will need a solid piece of evidence or very strong witness statement to prove this. For example: the dog was removed from the yard, and the lock on the gate was cut with a bolt cutter; or a witness saw someone enter your property the day the dog went missing, and he or she can identify the type of car or other identifying criteria or evidence.
- Get the name and badge number of the officer taking your report and ask who the detective will be. Be firm but friendly. Do not get aggressive or threatening in any way. You need their help. Do not intimidate but instead encourage the detective's involvement in your case.
- It is best if the detective will come out to take the police report where the dog was stolen. If the police insist on taking the report over the phone or having you come in the station to make the report, it is very likely that the police will not be able to devote much time to the case. If this is the case, consider hiring a private investigator in your area.
- Regardless of police participation, you can develop your own leads, but you need to encourage police intervention and check regularly with the officer or detective handling your case. Again, firm and friendly is the name of the game, but so is persistent. Do not be surprised or discouraged if the police inform you that they cannot devote time to this type of theft as they have a heavy caseload, which is usually very true. That said, you have a missing family member, and at the very least she is stolen property, so you are correct in expecting cooperation.
- There is always the media who may have an interest in the theft of a dog, but this can be very tricky.

If you believe you know where your stolen pet is being kept: It is imperative that you do *not* approach the individual or the property where you feel the dog is being harbored. Call the police and explain that you need their help to knock on the door, because you fear for your safety. If the police will not come, do *not* go on the property. Usually if you have kept in touch with the detective, a patrol officer will go to the location, if for no other reason than he or she does not want you injured on his or her watch.

> **Hire a private investigator, "PI", licensed in the state** where your pet went missing. Select an investigator who is passionate about your case, knows the area, and preferably has handled the recovery

of stolen property, which is what a stolen pet is legally considered in most states. Although it is beneficial to work with an investigator who specializes in missing pets and has a tracking-dog team, it is not a requirement, as there are very few PIs who do this work. Much of the work on this type of case will be witness, lead development, and surveillance.

- Be sure you understand what the PI can do for you.
- Most PIs work on an hourly basis with a retainer up front. It is best to set a "not to exceed" fee so you know what you will be spending. If the cost gets near the expected set fee, then the PI can notify you, and you can decide if you would like more investigative work done at that time. Do not leave an open check or credit card without a written contract of a "not to exceed" fee.
- Make sure the PI is clear with you on when the investigation will begin, dates, and so on. Enforce that time is of the essence and this is an emergency.
- *Important*: There is a current trend in the missing-pet industry for people calling themselves pet detectives to work lost-pet cases. Unless these people are licensed private investigators, they cannot help you on a stolen-animal case. In all states, they need to be licensed even if they think they do not. Use a licensed professional trained in witness and lead development, surveillance, and recovery. A pet detective or other such unlicensed individual does not have the training, skills, or legal ability.

You now need to proceed with a **community-awareness campaign**, pronto. The more people who know your dog is missing, the better.

And remember this: to the police, your dog is stolen; to everyone else, he is missing.

Many people will not want to get involved with a stolen-dog case, so I encourage you to say your dog is missing. Blasting the public and social media with "stolen dog" does not work very often and causes people who might otherwise help choose not to get involved. Your dog is missing.

If at any time you find that your dog was not stolen or you learn he has been turned loose, then proceed as below.

First and foremost, get to the shelter or animal-control agency immediately to report the new information. Get signs up and then follow the steps below based on the timing.

Developing the strategy

Unless you absolutely know someone has stolen your dog, you must cover all the bases until one scenario can be pursued. So follow the most likely scenarios first.

- Keep a **sightings journal**. I recommend that you respond to sightings immediately. When a dog has been rescued, there may not be any sightings, as the dog was picked up very quickly. In other cases, neighbors, passersby, and even relatives of the rescuers give information that leads to the return of the dog.

- **Develop witnesses** as you would for any other scenario near the point of escape for sightings, information, and leads. If you receive a sightings call or someone states that his or her neighbor, acquaintance, and so on has a new dog that looks like yours, then you need to proceed cautiously. Sometimes you can knock on the door, and the rescuer will hand you your dog. Sometimes it can be more difficult.
- Use a **neighborhood grid search**.
- Create a **photo identification lineup** card to help confirm that the dog the witnesses see is in fact your dog.

Community-awareness campaign

- Purchase or make the **community-awareness signs**. *Do not* put "stolen dog" on these. Your dog is missing. Get these up as soon as possible. We are looking for anyone who has seen your dog to call and possibly "give up the thief" or the person who now has the dog. Rewards are very important in stolen-dog cases. Place signs at the point last seen and also near anywhere where you feel the dog may be. Be careful; do not go off on a tangent.
- Proceed to **flyers** as calling cards.
- Place an **ad in the newspaper**. See the instructions for written ads and ads for a rescued pet.
- **Post** on lost-and-found websites and missing-pet alert groups. The ads and postings should include locations last seen.
- **Social media**: Post your missing dog to your Facebook profile and encourage others to share the post. If your dog is gone longer than forty-eight hours, a Facebook page can be helpful. Instagram and other social media platforms can be helpful also. Remember to be careful here. Posting your dog as stolen is a double-edged sword; it creates great interest but can also create ambivalence with some people who may have information but do not want to get involved.
- **Media involvement**: Consider this option carefully before you proceed. If there is something unique about your case beyond the dog being stolen, then media involvement might be beneficial. The story angle should have something to do with your dog and her presence in your life.

There are additional instructions and suggestions at http://www.howtofindalostdog.org/more-about-the-nine-scenarios.html.

The Dog That Meets with an Accident

This scenario includes all dogs that meet with an accident, and the accident is the reason the dog is missing. The most common accident a dog might encounter is a collision with a car. This scenario includes any situation that results in a pet having an accident that may incapacitate him or ultimately cause his death.

Profiling Query for a Dog That May Have Met with an Accident

Below are some of the factors to consider for this scenario.

1. Did your dog go missing at night?
2. Did you or anyone see or hear skidding tires, a crash, or a yelp during the time when your dog first went missing?
3. Does your dog have any of the STARS behaviors (shy, timid, aloof, reserved, or skittish)? Note: dogs with this behavior profile do not allow strangers to approach, and should they have a glancing blow with a car, they will most likely bolt and not allow help.
4. Is there a known toxic area nearby?
5. Is it possible there were pesticides being sprayed or set out and your dog found them?
6. Does your dog hunt for mice, moles, or gophers?
7. Did anyone notice the dog eating any type of plant or bush?
8. Is there an automobile-repair shop or auto repair going on near where your dog went missing? Note: many dogs will drink antifreeze, and although this is a rare occurrence, it should be considered if there is a possibility nearby.
9. Are there ponds, lakes, or large bodies of water in the area where the dog went missing?
10. Is there a known poisonous-snake population in the area where the dog went missing?
11. Was the dog's missing event caused by a tragic or traumatic escape event like an auto accident or other crisis that the dog was involved with?
12. In the area where the dog went missing, is there steep terrain or cliffs?

Profile

Any dog can fall victim to an accident, but some environmental situations and personality traits are more likely to produce this outcome. For example:

- The point of escape or point last seen is near a busy street, highway, turnpike, or freeway.
- The dog went missing in the early evening or when it was dark.
- Poisonous snakes are known to be in the area of the escape.
- The dog readily approaches small rodents and reptiles in play or aggression.
- The dog is *not* a finicky eater.
- The dog is not a good swimmer.
- Mice, snails, or scorpions are present, and poisons are put out by neighbors or others to combat them.
- Chemical poisons, coolant, and so on are accessible, and the pet is not a finicky eater.
- The dog is shy and frightened and tends to bolt and run when frightened.
- There are large bodies of water in the area that may or not be covered in ice.
- There are new or different plants in the house or yard. Poinsettia, tulips, azaleas, philodendron, English ivy, jade, and aloe vera are all toxic houseplants. Seasonal specialty plants are more likely to create an interest for a curious dog or one that chews a lot.
- There is an attractive nuisance area with dangerous elements in the area of point last seen.

Note: It is important to remember that some scenarios may present and look like others.

Characteristics, Sightings, and Leads

The following may be present in this scenario:

- There were no sightings of the pet near or heading toward any of the above nuisance or danger locations.
- The dog is not kept in a fenced yard and has free roaming access with a routine and known boundaries. The dog disappears without a trace.
- Honking or screeching of tires is heard by a witness or the pet owner near the time of the disappearance.
- Witnesses see a car stopped in the middle of the road or street near the point of escape or point last seen.
- A cat or dog fight is heard or seen at the time of the disappearance.
- Witnesses report that a neighbor is a "dog hater" or has been known or suspected of putting out poison.
- Pest or insecticide companies have recently been in the area.
- The dog was last seen near a body of water and has not been seen since.

- Lakes, ponds, and waterways are frozen.
- Fast-moving water is nearby.
- A unique or out-of-the-ordinary event occurred the day the dog went missing.

Case Study: Rudy

As told by Rudy's family:

"On January 29th at approximately 1:00 p.m., the mail-delivery person came to our business. This was earlier than normal, and I was at lunch while Phil was out playing golf.

We take our dogs to work with us Monday through Friday, and they keep us company in the front office. When the postal worker comes in, she always feeds the dogs one biscuit each. On this fateful day, after she gave each dog a biscuit, she opened the door and went out but this time all three of our dogs followed her out the door! This had never happened before.

An employee brought Dutch and Cappy back, but Rudy wouldn't come to her. He just kept on going! Another employee ran after him (which we know is the wrong thing to do). Rudy was worried and may have questioned, "Why is this person chasing after me and screaming?" So of course, he started to go faster, and the employee couldn't keep up with him. She last saw him turning south along the access road of a major highway called Central Expressway.

The rest of the story is reconstructed based on witnesses. We believe that Rudy kept on traveling south until he got to Mockingbird Lane, a major eight lane artery in Dallas. We believe that Rudy may have crossed Mockingbird and was then hit by a car.

On Wednesday night around 10:00 p.m., a Good Samaritan saw Rudy in the parking lot of The Palomar Hotel. He got out of his car and tried to catch Rudy, but the now injured dog was so terrified, he just ran away. Luckily the man was able to follow Rudy and saw him head toward an empty lot behind the hotel. He then lost sight of Rudy. It would be days before we knew about this sighting and this man's efforts to help Rudy.

In the meantime, Phil and I searched and put flyers up every day. Unfortunately, we soon found out that as soon as we put them up, someone was taking them down. Phil said it was probably the telephone company since we had nailed them to telephone poles. This was incredibly discouraging to me, and I cried every time I saw where a flyer had been taken down.

We got a few calls, but none were Rudy. We then called private investigator Karin TarQwyn and asked for her help. We were tired and discouraged and sure that someone had found Rudy and was keeping him in their house. Karin assured us that this was probably not the case but that instead he was roaming. She designed a strategy that included a public-awareness campaign. We got a call from a dog rescuer who had seen the posters designed by Karin, and she told Phil that they were the best posters she'd ever seen!

Finally, the man who sighted Rudy saw one of the posters Saturday at 10:00 p.m. when he came out of a movie. He immediately called Phil's cell phone, but we were asleep, exhausted from the mental stress and from putting up the new posters all day. We didn't hear the message until Sunday morning when we woke up.

We immediately drove to the area described by the caller and started calling Rudy's name. Off in the distance, a pair of ears popped up from behind a pile of rubble. It was Rudy, and as Phil started to walk toward him, he became terrified and didn't recognize him, (as Karin had said might happen). The hair on the back of Rudy's neck was up, he tucked his tail and started to run away at full speed, but something was very wrong—he was dragging his leg. I called Rudy, and while he looked at me, he didn't come to me. Our other dogs were with us, and I calmly but quickly got Cappy out of the car. I said, "Look, Rudy, it's Cappy!" Rudy looked over at Cappy. He slowly and carefully came toward us. By now I was crying and repeating Rudy's name over and over. He finally came up to Cappy, and I collapsed in joy. It had been such an ordeal.

Rudy was obviously injured, so we immediately took him to the Emergency Clinic. He was diagnosed with a broken femur and severe dehydration; the vet said he was 60 percent dehydrated. Rudy had surgery on Monday at the Veterinary Specialists Center where they had to put two pins in his busted-up leg.

I truly believe that if it wasn't for Karin's strategy, advice, and constant reassurance, Phil and I could not have made it through this. I know we wouldn't have Rudy back with us alive. We are very thankful we made that call".

Phil & Deirdre M.—Dallas, Texas

Actions and Activities to Pursue

The following are the actions and activities suggested for this scenario. The techniques and actions suggested are described in detail in **Section 3: Actions, Activities, and Techniques.**

- **First-response protocol** in the first hours.
- **Ground-zero search** of home or point of escape (unless pet is known to have left, and it is *confirmed*).
- **Witness development** near point of escape or point last seen for sightings, information, and leads that may reveal an accident or other incident.
- **Hire a professional with tracking dogs** if you believe your pet has met with an accident and is injured and at large or hiding. The earlier the K9s can get out, the better the chances of recovering an injured pet.
- **Check emergency animal hospitals** ASAP by phone.
- **Neighborhood grid search** unless you have a confirmed sighting out of the area.
- **Check animal shelters**, humane societies, and so on for dead-on-arrival or injured animals brought in matching your pet's physical description and approximate location.
- **Check dead animal removal service** in the area for animals and locations that may match your pet's situation.
- **Tiger Line Physical Search** for evidence of an injured pet, blood, or remains if deceased.
- **Signage** for sightings and for information about the accident if you have reliable evidence that the pet has been injured. If you are in question as to whether your pet has met with an accident, sign as normal for any information.
- **Flyers** to hand to people as a calling card when you are searching and developing witnesses and sightings. If you have reliable evidence that the pet has met with an accident, post flyers and develop witnesses near the accident site to ascertain the pet's direction of travel after the accident.

There are additional instructions and suggestions at http://www.howtofindalostdog.org/more-about-the-nine-scenarios.html.

The Dog Experiencing
Confusion, Illness, or Pain (CIP)

This dog may be confused and wandering or hiding, resting, collapsed or sedated in an area distant from his home or point of escape.

Profiling Query for a Dog That May Go Missing Due to CIP

Determining factors: Below are some of the factors to consider for this scenario.

In this scenario it is not necessary to have a "yes" on 50 percent of the questions. If your dog experienced different or difficult behavior immediately before going missing, this scenario is possible.

1. Was the dog behaving abnormally prior to disappearing?
2. Has the dog recently been given a new medication or experienced a change in dosage?
3. Did the dog experience *any* type of accident prior to going missing?
4. Is the dog missing in an area that he is unfamiliar with?
5. Does this dog run or hide when frightened?
6. Is the climate unusually warm or hot?
7. Has the dog been diagnosed with an illness or disease?
8. Did your dog disappear without a trace?
9. Is your dog missing near a heavily wooded area or large open space?
10. Are there physical factors in the area that would make it easy for a dog to hide and not be seen?

The most common dogs to react to illness and hide are older dogs and shy dogs, as well as dogs that have just had medical treatment, are on a new medication, or recently had an injury - especially a head injury.

This dog is missing because it felt poorly and has wandered away and is in hiding; the dog is unable or unwilling to respond. Contrary to popular belief, I do not believe pets go off to die. It is more probable that animals hide in an attempt to get away from anything that will disturb them. Unfortunately, when they go into hiding like this, they most likely need medical attention.

This scenario is not to be confused with a dog that has become injured or sick as a result of its escaping. The dog in this scenario is already confused, ill, or in pain before disappearing regardless whether the pet owner realizes it.

Profile

Any pet can react, lie low, or hide because it is ill or confused. Although it is most common with cats, I have known dogs to pursue this behavior also, particularly the older and chronically ill canine. The criteria below can be present in this scenario.

- A dog that is known to be ill or on new medication.
- Any pet that routinely hides when alarmed, frightened, or feeling unwell.
- Dogs with a low tolerance for pain or discomfort.
- A dog that was recently spayed or neutered or underwent a surgery where anesthesia was used.
- Canines that have exhibited "bolt and hide" behavior before.
- Before the disappearance, the pet owner may have noticed a change in attitude, behavior or activity, even if subtle.
- There has been a change in elimination routine—anything different from the norm, even accidents in the house when the dog never had accidents.
- The pet has disappeared, and the pet owner has no idea how or when. Unlike cats, dogs usually exhibit illness or feelings of being sick. They may go to an area outside of the house to be left alone—not to die alone, as is popular theory.

Characteristics, Sightings, and Leads

- Dogs that are confused may run until they can't continue and will then lie down.
- Dogs can travel a fair distance when scared and confused depending on the severity of the injury. Many whimper very quietly or utter no sound at all.
- A sick dog will generally not travel far.
- Witnesses may have seen the dog lying in a public area or roadside appearing sick or injured.
- The pet owner notices vomit, bloody feces, or other body fluids near the point last seen.
- The area is experiencing heat and high temperatures, and the dog does not tolerate this well and seeks a cool, damp place to recover.
- The dog is left without access to water.

Case Study: Angelo

As told by his family:

"Officially, he's CH. Marchello's Royal Guardian HIC—an eight-year-old Smooth Coated Collie with successes in the confirmation ring, a certification in herding, experience in therapy, and my daughter Sarah's Junior Showmanship dog. He's far better known as Angelo and more important than any titles he's earned is that he's an essential part of our family and we love him more than practically anything.

Angelo's story begins with me applying a topical flea and tick medication on him and his having a bad reaction to it. He was sick all night long and into the next day as well. For some dogs, a matter such as this would just take time to get over, but Angelo has a history of small GI issues turning into serious problems, which has landed him in the emergency clinic, so we never treat anything lightly.

We left him in the care of my son Matt, who took him out mid-day and left him unattended for a moment. When he returned Angelo had vanished. I was at work and couldn't leave. My husband Steve left work early and came home to search. Sarah joined the hunt as soon as she got home from school. When I pulled into the driveway five hours after he had last been seen and no one ran out to greet me, shouting, "He's been found!" my heart sank, because I knew how serious this situation would be. Angelo is not allowed to roam, but the times he has escaped, he was always found within twenty minutes either by us or by a neighbor. For Angelo to be missing for five hours was unimaginable. We are surrounded by swamps and deep woods covered with thick undergrowth this time of year. Angelo could have been lying anywhere in need of medical attention.

We searched into the dark and turned up nothing. Sarah and I went out with a flashlight, trying to see the reflections of his eyes, and gave up after about an hour. Reluctantly we went home, leaving Angelo outside and by himself for the first time in his life.

Needless to say, we didn't sleep well that night—Friday dawned with a need to make up lost dog flyers and distribute them to Vets, local shelters, and neighbors. We began our search again finding nothing. It was if he had never existed at all.

I have to admit it was not my idea to contact Karin. A good friend, who owns Dachshunds, suggested the tracking idea and made a connection to Jordina Thorp somehow. Jordina provided my friend with Karin's information, and she in turn passed Karin's number on to me.

Several things struck me when I first called Karin—she was a calming influence in a situation that for me had gotten out of control. She was able to analyze what facts I could give her and combine them with topographical maps she pulled up on the Internet and was able to offer predictions on what might have happened—the wild card was Angelo being ill. Having just gone through this first hand with her lead dog Cade, Karin was very sensitive to how this malady can totally change a scenario. She agreed to meet with me and Sarah the next day to try and find

Angelo. It poured that night, and the winds were high—very distressing—but we went to sleep that night believing that we might at least find some closure the next day.

Karin and Jordina showed up at 11:00 a.m. on Saturday—Angelo had been now missing for forty-eight hours. She first brought Cade out—a lab/coonhound mix. This would be Cade's first case since his illness, and we weren't sure how good his stamina would be. Karin presented him with Angelo's scent article—a fabric clown collar he had worn in Sarah's high-school production of *Twelfth Night* in which he had been featured last fall—and Cade immediately started pulling Karin in the direction Angelo had reportedly last been seen in. He led her deep into the woods, over a stone wall, and into a farmer's field. We were now past the point any of us had searched because we were so convinced that Angelo was sick or dying. When Cade scaled the side of a granite face and scrambled onto the rise above it, I was hard pressed to believe Angelo was capable of ascending such a vertical climb, but Karin mentioned that since Cade tracks the air the routes he takes are not always the ones the dog he's tracking would have taken. We paused by a shed where we saw dried muddy footprints, which might have been Angelo's. It heartened me to think he had spent a night under shelter. Cade led us down a driveway where he seemed to start losing Angelo's scent a bit.

At this point, to give Cade a break and to confirm the trail he had shown us, Karin had us go back to my house and begin the journey all over again, this time using Brodie, a German wire-haired pointer, who tracks by ground scent. Brodie led Karin out in the same direction, and his path was exactly what Cade's had been. I can't tell you the feeling I got seeing two completely different dogs using two completely different methods of tracking determine where my beloved dog I thought was dead had traveled. I was exhilarated—for the first time in two days, I thought there was a good chance Angelo was still alive.

Cade got switched back in and led us to the next town, and unfortunately straight onto a trail that put Angelo on the Metro North Train tracks—one of the busiest train corridors on the East Coast. Brodie confirmed Angelo's scent to the tracks. So did Nash, a beagle cross, as did Trump, a Jack Russell Terrier. All the optimism I had been feeling left me, and I was certain Angelo had met his fate on those tracks. The same friend who found Karin for me had lost her Lab on that exact same stretch of tracks the year before. Jordina and Brodie tracked alongside of the tracks for a short period of time, but soon the sides of the tracks closed in, and it wasn't safe to track any more.

At this point I was all set to just walk the tracks by myself because if Angelo had died there, I needed to know that and wanted to retrieve his remains. Karin suggested we try to get a better idea how far down the tracks his scent went first so that I did not have to look in areas he had not been to. We drove alongside the tracks, and as soon as Karin saw a trestle over the marsh, her gut feeling was that Angelo would not have crossed such a structure. That assumption proved correct—Cade was not able to detect Angelo's scent past that point, and we back tracked until he picked up his scent again, now knowing exactly how far Angelo had been on the tracks without putting handlers and dogs in danger. I am still in awe that Cade is able to detect a scent in the air a quarter mile away—it's just mind boggling but I witnessed it myself.

We parted ways with a clear plan—I would first check the tracks to see if Angelo was there. Sarah and I went back home and brought Steve and Matt with us to search the tracks. We walked on one side of the tracks, Matt and Steve the other, and it was a pretty grim experience for us. It seemed surreal that a dog that had been so carefully attended to his whole life would have it end on railroad tracks a mile away from his home. Fortunately, we didn't find him, which gave me hope again that our boy was alive.

Karin's e-mails started arriving as soon as she got back home. How she had the stamina to do more work after the physical workout we had endured all day plus the six hours it took her to drive to Connecticut and back, I'll never know, but the first one contained the redesigned signage, and it was fantastic. So professional! The next e-mail showed the routes each of the dogs had taken that day, and subsequent e-mails showed where signs needed to be placed and would effectively circle the area that our boy had been tracked to. Probably for the first time in more than two days, I finally felt that things were under control, and once we got these signs up in the right areas, people would start calling us with Angelo sightings. I went to sleep that third night hopeful for the first time.

The call from a neighboring farmer came Sunday at 9:00 a.m. Angelo had been found by his daughter, who clipped a horse lead to his collar and effectively ended our nightmare. We drove to him and immediately and picked him up, a little dirty, a bit dazed from three days on his own, but really no worse for the wear. I woke Sarah up that morning with her chum at her bedside, gently prodded her, and when she turned over I said, "Someone's here to see you." I'll never forget the look on her face—initially disbelief and then pure joy! He will never be let off leash again, and a microchip is in his near future. As I write this, he is resting comfortably at my feet.

Karin was able to take an unpredictable, emotional situation and steady it using techniques she has honed over time. She understands not only her dogs, but I was amazed how much better she knew Angelo in some ways than I did. She obviously loves what she does and is passionate about it as well- compassionate about what we were going through too. She was someone to lean on when I desperately needed someone to lead the way, and it's hard to put into words what that meant at the time. There are never any guarantees in anything like this, but even if we had had the misfortune of finding Angelo dead, it would have given us the closure we wouldn't have had otherwise.

Happily, we were extremely lucky; our treasured boy is home with us where he belongs!

Thank you Karin, Jordina, Cade, Brodie, Nash, Trump, and Paco from the bottom of our hearts. We will never forget what you did for us—Never!

Diane, Sarah, Steve, Matt, and Angelo M.—Fairfield, Connecticut"

Actions and Activities to Pursue

The following are the actions and activities suggested for this scenario. The techniques and actions suggested are described in detail in **Section 3: Actions, Activities, and Techniques.**

- **First-response protocol** in the first hours.
- **Ground-zero search** of home or point of escape (unless pet is known to have left and it is confirmed).
- **Witness development** near point of escape for sightings, information, and leads. Mention that your pet may be ill and lying low or hiding.
- **Check emergency animal hospitals** by phone.
- **Neighborhood grid search** for older dogs or dogs that are ill prior to disappearance (unless you have confirmed sightings out of the area).
- **Tiger Line Physical Search**: see the activity instructions, and be aware you are looking for evidence that is best seen within eighteen inches of the ground—basically knee level.
- **Check animal shelters**, humane societies, and so on. Check the injured stray and hospital sections of the facilities.
- **Sign** for sightings at the point of escape and at all confirmed sightings or sightings where you are in question as to whether it was your pet that was seen. When in doubt, hang more signs.
- **Flyers** to hand to people as a calling card when you are searching and developing witnesses and sightings.
- **Spotlighting**: this is one of the rare occasions when the use of a spotlight is helpful in finding a dog.
- **Hire a professional with tracking dogs (K9s)** if you feel your pet may have met this situation. Professionally trained scent-specific tracking K9s are trained to follow the pet's scent even if hiding. If a pet has lain in an area for a substantial length of time, the scent will be very concentrated in that area, making it easier for a trained team to find.

There are additional instructions and suggestions at http://www.howtofindalostdog.org/more-about-the-nine-scenarios.html.

The Dog That Is Accidentally Transported

These pets are unable to respond and return home because they have accidentally entered a vehicle or object that has moved and is now in another place outside their home territory. We have known cats to jump in the repair mans' van, as well as cat that boarded a mobile home before it was moved three states away. This scenario is more common with curious cats but we have known dogs to find themselves in this situation. One dog entered the rear door of a bread-delivery truck while a delivery was being made. These pets are generally curious in nature and have no problem entering vehicles and other interesting spaces that ultimately change location. Another circumstance that more commonly occurs is when a pet is inside a vehicle that is taken or stolen and then released when the driver or thief realizes the animal is on board.

Profiling Query for a Dog That May Have Been Accidentally Transported

Determining factors: Below are some of the factors to consider for this scenario.

This is the rarest situation a dog may encounter in the Nine Scenarios. This should only be considered as a strong possibility if your dog has jumped into a strange vehicle before.

1. Does this dog love to ride in vehicles?
2. Would the dog jump into a vehicle it does not know?
3. Was the weather warm when the pet went missing when vehicle windows might have been down?
4. Is there a train station, utility or bus station, or lot with commercial transport or freight vehicles nearby?
5. Was anyone moving during the time your dog went missing?
6. Were there construction or other vehicles in your neighborhood when the dog was last seen?
7. Have there been any confirmed sightings of the dog that are several miles away and there is no explanation as to how the dog could have got there?

Profile

The following characteristics are most common with this scenario.

- The curious and outgoing pet that is always into something.
- Dogs that have frequent outdoor access.
- Pets that readily get into or lie on top of cars, trucks, or vans without fear.
- Pets that disappear when weather is warm and car windows are down.
- A train station nearby with open freight cars.
- Neighbors are moving, and moving-van doors are left open and unattended.
- Construction, or a repairman's vehicle, school bus, or other service vehicle parked in the area.
- Neighbors are moving or going on vacation and leave doors to a van, trailer, or camper open.

Sightings and Leads

The following leads and sightings may be in evidence:

- There are no sightings in the local area.
- May have sightings farther away that the owner may discount, because the pet could not have traveled that far on its own.
- Upon questioning, a witness alerts the pet owner of service or transport vehicles in the area.
- Rumor or sightings of a pet jumping out of a vehicle.
- Someone calls from a distance and explains that "this dog just showed up here."

Case Study: Ricky

The accidental transport of a dog is very rare, but when it does happen, it is usually because, like Ricky, the dog was in a car waiting for his family to return. In the interim, a thief or group of kids comes upon the car and steals it, most likely unaware that the dog is in the car. Such was the case of Ricky, a small Maltese mix.

Ricky was in his crate in the backseat of the family Mercedes waiting for his family to return from a restaurant. They were in the restaurant for an hour, and when they returned, their car was gone.

Interested only in Ricky's return, the family focused all their efforts on the return of their dog and not their car. Ricky's crate and leash were found in an alley about six miles away. There was a lot of public assistance in this case, and the sightings, both valid and invalid, were many.

It is believed that Ricky was turned loose somewhere near where his crate was found, but this was never confirmed, as we did not travel to the site to work the case on location.

The men who stole the car were found and arrested, but the only information they gave was that they had turned the dog loose when they realized he was in the car. The location was never ascertained as their story changed several times. There was no benefit to them if they told the truth, there was no lesser punishment offered for the truth, so they had no motivation and were most likely told by their attorneys not to participate unless they were awarded a lesser sentence or a deal was made. This did not happen, as Ricky was just a dog to the legal system.

The search went on for several months, and I consulted on it several times, but again I did not go out with the K9 team as the costs for us to travel that great a distance was prohibitive for all parties. Had I gone out, we would have scanned the homes of the thieves and their neighborhood, the area where the crate was found, and the area Ricky was taken from in case they really did open the door and let him out right away as the thieves said they did. Due to the media attention, inexperienced handlers and new pet detectives volunteered their services, and they did not have the experience to handle such a case. The evidence went nowhere, and Ricky was never found.

Actions and Activities to Pursue

The following are the actions and activities suggested for this scenario. The techniques and actions suggested are described in detail in **Section 3: Actions, Activities, and Techniques.**

- **First-response protocol** in the first hours.
- **Ground-zero search** of home or point of escape (unless the pet is known to have left, and it is confirmed).
- **Witness development** near point of escape for sightings, information, and leads. Inquire after the suspected vehicle by calling the company that sent the vehicle and neighbor that requested the work if applicable.
- **Check emergency animal hospitals** by phone.
- **Neighborhood grid search** for older dogs and cats (unless you have confirmed sightings out of the area).
- **Check animal shelters**, humane societies, and so on.
- **Place Signage** for sightings at the point of escape and at all confirmed sighting locations or those locations where you are in question as to whether it was your pet that was seen. Sign near the company headquarters or office if commercial vehicle transport is suspected. When in doubt, hang more signs.
- **Make Flyers** to hand to people as a calling card when you are searching and developing witness and sightings. Flyers are to hand to people, and signs are to post for maximum exposure.
- **Run ad in newspaper with dates, times, and even suspected vehicle**, if appropriate.
- **Social media**: Post this missing dog's plight to your Facebook profile and encourage others to share the post. If your dog is gone longer than forty-eight hours, a Facebook page can be helpful. Instagram and other social media platforms can be helpful also.
- **Hire a professional with tracking dogs** if you feel your pet may have met this situation. Professionally trained K9s are trained to scan areas where the dog may have gotten out of the vehicle and alert if the pet's scent is in the area.

There are additional instructions and suggestions at http://www.howtofindalostdog.org/more-about-the-nine-scenarios.html.

The Dog That Is Intentionally Displaced or Removed

This dog has been unable to return home because it has been displaced from the area intentionally. Pets in this situation may have been trapped or caught by a neighbor and taken away, caught as a stray by animal control and transported to the local or not-so-local animal shelter, caught by a local dog or cat hoarder or collector, or even removed secretly by a family member or friend. However it happened, the pet was removed intentionally and is unable to return home.

Profiling Query for a Dog That Has Been Intentionally Displaced

Determining factors: Below are some of the factors to consider for this scenario.

1. Is this dog gregarious and outgoing?
2. Will the dog allow a stranger to approach?
3. If the dog has been missing before, has someone else ever returned the dog?
4. Does the dog have any disturbing or nuisance behaviors?
5. Has anyone in the area ever complained about the dog or its behaviors?
6. Is there a family member or friend who does not like the dog or has complained about the dog?
7. Is the dog one of the breeds that some people may feel are dangerous or aggressive?
8. Was the dog dirty, unkempt, matted or left unsheltered when he went missing?
9. Was the dog tied out on a chain or tether?
10. Have other dogs or pets been reported missing in the area?
11. Is there anyone in the family who may have ill will and is capable of removing the animal?

Profile

- Any pet can experience this situation, but the most likely pet is one that someone feels is causing a disturbance or causing the person a problem:
- Dogs that bark a lot or jump at the fence when someone walks by.

58

- Areas where there are very few stray dogs and Animal Control is readily called or alerted.
- Outdoor dogs that regularly roam or go into the yards of others.
- Situation where a family member or close friend does not like the pet or feels it should not be at the residence.
- Dogs that someone may feel are a danger to the neighborhood. This is a common feeling with many breeds, with the pit bull type leading the list.
- Dogs that get out frequently and roam on the property of others, ("the escape artists").
- A pet that someone may feel is being neglected or mistreated by its owner or someone in the area (whether true or not).
- An unusual number of pets missing recently in the area.
- Areas where there are homeowners who are particular about their landscaping, garden, or lawns.
- Location where there is an aggressive child with a suspected history of cruelty. This is the rarest of situations, but there is a definite profile for these adolescents and teenagers.
- Witnesses may report rumor or knowledge of a neighbor with a humane trap.
- Revenge can also be in this category but differs from the stolen pet in that the pet is not removed from its property but is in a public place or on the property of another.

Characteristics, Sightings, and Leads

- A pet that usually returns does not, which is unusual and out of the ordinary.
- Animal Control or a dog catcher was seen in the area.
- No sightings after day of disappearance.
- Witnesses share their suspicions of cat or dog hater.
- Family member, neighbor, or friend is indifferent or wants immediate acceptance that the pet is gone and not returning. Get over it. Not willing to participate in search.

Case Study: Rocky

The most common incident of intentional displacement is the dog that is picked up as a stray or nuisance by animal control.

When Jill returned home that first night and saw the gate swinging in the breeze, initially she was not panicked. Rocky, her adventurous Jack Russell terrier, was trained to never go beyond the third house to the left, and she felt sure his training had held.

Reality set in when she entered the front door and called out to the little adventurer, and he did not come as he usually did. She was shocked and ran out the door to begin driving the neighborhood calling for him. She would later find out that a new meter reader had entered her yard and left the gate open—something she had never thought of. She took her own readings and sent them to the utility company herself. A new employee was not in her realm of possibilities.

She also had wrongly assumed that Rocky was trained to not go beyond the third house to the left when in fact she was trained...not Rocky. They had a "gentleman's agreement," so to speak, that she would call him when he reached the third house, and he would turn around and run back for affection and treats in celebration. Without Jill there to call him, he had eventually wandered away.

Rocky had been missing three days when we arrived. The dog team immediately tracked Rocky to the left, as he had always gone, but then continued across the street and to the west. We followed the little terrier's scent up one street and down the other for two hours until Cade stopped dead in his tracks, lifted his head to test the air, and turned abruptly north, running down the middle of the street. After about a half mile, I pulled him up and told the pet owner that we should concentrate our efforts back where we had been tracking earlier. I did not know what Cade was doing, but I felt sure the little dog had not run down the middle of the street, or he would have been killed.

Meanwhile, earlier that same morning, a woman had noticed a small terrier hanging around her house. She gave the little dog water and then decided it best to call Animal Control to come and pick him up. They came around eleven and put Rocky in the truck's cage compartment in the rear. The officers continued on their way and finished out their day before returning to the shelter. Later, when she went to the grocery store, the woman who had called animal control saw our signs and called Jill to tell her what had transpired.

We would later discover that Cade had been tracking Rocky's scent as he was riding in the Animal Control truck's outdoor compartment. Rocky's scent was escaping through the wide-open ventilation vents, creating a trail down the middle of every street the truck drove down. The dog team was less than a quarter mile from the woman's house where Animal Control had picked up the little dog. The truck had transported Rocky down the very street where Cade had been running down the middle of the street. Lesson learned: always trust the nose of the tracking dogs!

Actions and Activities to Pursue

The following are the actions and activities suggested for this scenario. The techniques and actions suggested are described in detail in **Section 3: Actions, Activities, and Techniques.**

- **First-response protocol** in the first hours.
- **Ground-zero search** of home or point of escape (unless the pet is known to have left, and it is confirmed).
- **Witness development** near point of escape for sightings, information, and leads. Pay close attention to neighbors and anyone suspected of possibly removing the animal.
- **Check emergency animal hospitals** by phone.
- **Neighborhood grid search** (unless you have confirmed sightings out of the area).
- **Check animal shelters**, humane societies, and so on. Many times a dog off its property is "picked up" by the Animal Control Agency in the area. Also, if someone intentionally removes a pet from the area, he or she may just take it to the shelter. Generally, the animal is taken to a different shelter than the local agency or a shelter or to a rescue out of the area where the pet owner might not typically look.
- **Signage** for sightings and information at the point of escape. When in doubt, sign it!
- **Flyers** to hand to people as a calling card when you are searching and developing witnesses, information, and sightings. Flyers are to hand to people, and signs are to post for maximum exposure. *Do not* put anything on the flyer stating that you suspect theft or intentional displacement. Sometimes people will be reluctant to get involved if they feel they may be in conflict with another neighbor.

There are additional instructions and suggestions at http://www.howtofindalostdog.org/more-about-the-nine-scenarios.html.

The Dog That Is Accidentally Trapped

This pet has wandered or fallen into a situation where he has become trapped and cannot get out.

Profiling Query for a Dog That Has Been Accidentally Trapped

Determining factors: Below are some of the factors to consider for this scenario.

This is an uncommon scenario, but it does happen on occasion.

1. Does this dog have free access to areas outside his property?
2. Is this dog an explorer or very curious?
3. Did the dog go missing with a leash, line, or rope attached?
4. Does the dog have unusually long hair and/or a low tolerance for pain?
5. Are there attractive nuisances or dangerous conditions in the area where the dog was last seen?
6. Has the dog ever been trapped or stuck before?
7. Do the homes in the area have basement window wells that can be accessed from the outside?
8. Will your dog go into dark areas willingly (such as a cave or basement)?

The most common of these is the pet that wanders into the neighbor's garage or shed while the door is open and then becomes trapped when the unknowing neighbor closes the door. Dogs are known to become trapped in sheds, storm drains, outhouses, abandoned buildings, and even discarded kitchen cabinets. We had one long-haired spaniel that became trapped in a briar bush two blocks from home. She stayed there in the bush for five days until she was found. She did not bark or make any noise, as is common with many pets.

This possibility should always be looked into when a pet that normally has outdoor access does not return as usual and there is a nuisance danger that could encourage this situation.

Profile

Any pet can become trapped, but curious dogs are the most likely to end up in this situation.

- Pet that is curious and an explorer type and likes to explore new places and things.
- Dogs may go through an open door or into a small or dark opening to check it out or hide.
- A skittish or xenophobic pet might pursue a hiding place in fright and become trapped.
- Any animal that readily hides when frightened is also a candidate.
- Dogs that regularly travel or have the opportunity to roam near mines, sump holes, drainage ditches, abandoned buildings, or wrecking and junk yards.
- Homes in the area have basements with belowground window boxes.
- Dog went missing with rope or leash attached.

Characteristics, Sightings, and Leads

- The dog may normally have outdoor access and goes out of his routine of returning home.
- No sightings other than maybe the first day.
- Neighbors or nearby businesses had doors open, or work was being done on the day of disappearance.
- Someone was moving or cleaning out a garage, basement, or shed on the day of disappearance.
- A neighbor went to mow a lawn, leaving a shed open for a period of time.
- For businesses, the most likely time a pet will become trapped is at closing time on a day the business is usually open.
- Hunters have set game traps in the area.
- A long-coated dog disappears in an area with thick brambles or briars.

Case Study: Abby

Abby, a Coton de Tulear, was dropped off to stay with friends while her family went on vacation. On the second day, she suddenly bolted out the front door and began to run through the unfamiliar neighborhood.

Her guardians gave chase, trying to keep the fleeing dog in sight. As she came to an intersection, she suddenly disappeared and was not seen again. Her guardians called her family, who flew home to join in the search. Abby had been staying with the fire-department chief and his family, so firefighters from all over came in to help find the little dog. Helicopters, heat-sensor cameras, and huge search parties spread out to try and find Abby. The little dog had just disappeared.

On day eleven of Abby's missing event, we were called in to help.

With no credible sightings, I started the dog team from Abby's point of escape. Lead dog Cade took scent and headed to the west. He tracked a half mile, crossing streets and checking for scent as he went. He steadily continued down a paved hillside.

Just before the third intersection, Cade stopped and turned back to a house on the east side of the street. He tried to get into the yard from street side but was unable to due to a steep drop-off.

On the night Abby disappeared, her caretakers had followed her and then lost sight of her in this very area. Cade wanted to go into the yard, so we knocked on the door. No one was home, but a friend of the homeowners decided to allow us to enter the property. We proceeded down the side yard, and Cade alerted toward the basement garage. I saw a flash of white, and a small dog clambered further into the basement and climbed up behind some old appliances. I brought the pet owner around and had him look in between the appliances. He excitedly said that yes, it was his Abby! I shut the pet owner and the dog inside the basement and waited. Within a few minutes, Abby came out from behind the junk to her happy dad. All was secured, and she was transported to the car and into the waiting arms of her family.

This story exemplifies how a STARS dog can go unnoticed. Based on Cade's work and Abby's sudden disappearance from the street, it is clear that Abby fell down the steep drop-off Cade had alerted near. The yard was a deep pit surrounded on all sides by tall and steep cliffs. Abby or any dog for that matter could not have gotten out of the yard.

All the yards and homes in this area were searched by Abby's family, friends, and the fire department with all their heat-sensing equipment and cameras. The basement where Cade found Abby was also searched. Abby had never made a sound when her family and the searchers were calling and searching for her nearby. In addition, the family at the home did not know the little dog was in their basement. Again it is important to remember that when a STARS dog goes missing, many times they hear but do not respond to their owner's calls or presence.

After she was missing for eleven days, it took Cade only twenty minutes to find Abby. When technology and human efforts failed, it was the nose of a dog that found her.

There are additional case studies on the website for this scenario.

Actions and Activities to Pursue

The following are the actions and activities suggested for this scenario. The techniques and actions suggested are described in detail in **Section 3: Actions, Activities, and Techniques.**

- **First-response protocol** in the first hours.
- **Ground-zero search** of home or point of escape (unless the pet is known to have left, and it is confirmed).
- **Witness development and neighborhood grid search**: This combined search takes on a more detailed effort than in any other scenario. The pet owner must think about objects or situations in the area that a dog could get into but not out of. Be aware of any neighbors who may have moved or had garage doors, sheds, or basement doors and windows open on the day of disappearance and then closed them. Check under houses, sheds, decks, abandoned cars and appliances, and in any dark area that could have been opened and then closed that is within your pet's regular territory. Use your inside voice with motivators (squeaky toys, clickers, etc.) to encourage a vocal response from the possibly trapped pet. If you discover neighbors who are out of town or have moved, and their leaving coincides with your pet's disappearance, question others to get the phone number or a cell phone for that individual or family.
- **Check emergency animal hospitals** by phone.
- **Hire a professional with tracking dogs** if you feel your pet may have met this situation. The K9s are trained to follow the pet's scent even if trapped. Note: Scent must be able to escape. In one of our cases, a cat fell to the bottom of a thirty-foot chimney in a vacant house. His scent did not travel up the chimney and was enclosed by all the brick, mortar, and metal.
- **Check animal shelters**, humane societies, and so on.
- **Post Signage** for sightings at the point of escape and at all confirmed sightings or sightings where you are in question as to whether it was your pet that was seen. We had a Labrador trapped in a basement and a Jack Russell stuck in a barn. Both dogs were recovered due to signs.
- **Create Flyers** to hand to people as a calling card when you are searching and developing witness and sightings.

There are additional instructions and suggestions at http://www.howtofindalostdog.org/more-about-the-nine-scenarios.html.

The Dog That Meets with a Predator

Any pet can meet with this situation, but some locations and animals will be more susceptible to this outcome.

Profiling Query for a Dog That May Have Met with a Predator

Determining factors: Below are some of the factors to consider for this scenario.

1. Are there predators in the area? (coyotes, foxes, owls, hawks, mountain lions, etc.).
2. Did the dog go missing without a trace (no sightings)?
3. Did the dog go missing in the early morning, late in the afternoon, or after dark?
4. Is the missing dog a small dog of less than twenty pounds?
5. Is the dog predominantly white in color?
6. Have other pets in the area gone missing and have not been found?
7. Did the dog go missing in a rural or forested area?
8. Was the dog older, in poor health, or in any way infirm or ill?
9. Did the dog suddenly bolt into the woods or open space as if chasing something and then was not seen or heard again?
10. Does this dog know his territory and always returns to his yard?

For years this was an occurrence that happened only to those who lived in the country or wilderness areas. That is not so anymore. As a society we have continued to develop excessive amounts of wilderness area, thus taking away the food sources of the animals and predators that live in these areas.

The most common predator today that may choose pets as prey is the coyote.

Coyotes are now found all over the country, as they no longer can restrict themselves to rural and wilderness areas. The coyote's primary food sources are moles, ground squirrels, rabbits, seeds, and berries. As our population continues to expand, adaptable predators like the coyote need to move into new areas to hunt and sustain life.

Other predators occasionally involved in choosing pets as prey are bobcats, foxes, mountain lions, bears, and fisher cats. Eagles, hawks, owls, and other birds of prey may also choose small pets as prey, although this is not a common occurrence.

Profile

Any pet can become the unexpected prey of a predator.

- The most likely candidates for a predator attack are dogs under twenty pounds or possibly a little larger depending on the area and the size of the predators in the environment. This, however, is not set in stone, as larger dogs do occasionally encounter this situation.
- In my experience, a higher percentage of white pets or pets with a significant amount of white on them meet this fate. The coyote is an opportunist, and it is possible that the white is a flag and easier to see.
- Pets may be older, ill or becoming ill, incapacitated, or blind. Those pets less physically capable seem to be more frequent targets.
- Pets that are in a high state of fear or that may have just become injured. They put off pheromones, (chemical substances which trigger an effect in other animals), and it is likely the predator is alerted to the release of these.

Characteristics, Sightings, and Leads

- Point of escape or point last seen may be in the country, woods, a pasture area, or a metro or subdivision that has a nearby greenbelt access, wilderness area, drainage-ditch system, or open space.
- Pet was last seen at night, in the late afternoon, or in the early morning.
- Pet left outside longer than normal.
- Point of escape or point last seen may be near or adjacent to a large storm-drain system that lets out into a wilderness or swamp area. Many pet owners are unaware of the origin and endings for these accesses. Coyotes use these extensively to travel, especially in places like Texas where the systems are large and easy to travel.
- There are no sightings of the pet, or maybe just one or two the first day the pet went missing.
- Coyotes or foxes have been seen or heard in the area. It is not necessary, however, to hear or see them for them to be in the area. Many pet owners have been shocked to learn they live among coyotes, because they have never heard them and felt that all coyotes howl. They do not.
- The pet goes missing at a time of year when coyotes are more actively pursuing alternate food sources such as in the winter when food sources are less and in the spring after females have had their cubs and there are now multiple mouths to feed.

Case Study: Yoshi

Yoshi's story is unique in many ways. Above all it brings to light the realistic outcomes that can be experienced in this situation. As skilled private investigators, we are not wizards with wands, just humans with compassion, skills, and awesome K9 partners.

The storm that hit Springfield, Missouri in spring of 2007 blew down trees, electrical lines, and the gate to the Howells' backyard, where two much-loved canine family members were frightened and spooked into the woods.

The treasured pooches were discovered missing within hours, and Shadow, the larger of the two canines, was found the next day. But the Howells knew their feisty six-pound Pomeranian, Yoshi, was in a perilous situation. As they struggled to control their panic and grief, the Howells searched for methods and suggestions to help them find the cherished pup.

After days of coaching by phone, the Howells asked us to bring in the dog team. From the beginning, it did not look good for the little dog. Lead dog Cade sprang into action immediately, following the little dog's scent trail straight into the woods. Upon entering the heavily wooded forests, the tracking-dog team followed a trail that went to a river that was now running swiftly due to the recent storms. Dodger alerted with a decomp or blood alert. Something had been injured or killed along the trail, and spirits sank. The dogs tracked a little further and then lost Yoshi's scent.

It appeared that Yoshi had met with a fox, as scat from a fox had been discovered along the trail the dog team was following. It was felt that Yoshi, at only six pounds, most likely had not survived. There was however a chance that he was alive, as we found no physical evidence of his demise. Also, the river was now higher than when Yoshi had gone missing, and the tracking dogs could not cross to the other side. The decision was made to leave the signage up to keep Yoshi in the forefront of the public's awareness.

That was a crucial decision. Two days later a jogger called to say she thought she had seen a small fluffy dog under a bridge in the area where Cade and Dodger had tracked. Although the Howells were doubtful, they decided it was worth a look.

As Ken arrived at the bridge, he noticed that the water was much lower now, but he still did not see a dog. He decided to wade into the river and approach the bridge from the riverside. As he waded up the river, a small puff of fur appeared and barked at him. He recognized the small bit of fluff as Yoshi. He waded closer and tried to approach him, but the injured dog backed up into an opening under the bridge and eluded capture. After some wrangling and corralling, Ken was able to get to Yoshi, grab him, and hang on. It was quickly apparent that Yoshi was severely injured, and Ken immediately headed to the emergency vet.

The vet found that Yoshi had in fact been attacked by a predator and had sustained a back injury. He was treated, shaved due to tick infestation, and released. He was back to his normal "silly behavior" within a month.

It is likely that due to the high tide of the river, Yoshi was up and under the bridge and could not get out due to the high water. The tracking dogs also could not get to the area and lost scent on the aft side of the bridge, as Yoshi was under the framework of the bridge, (which was underground and below the trail where the dog team was working).

Case Study: Princess

This story, although sad and graphic, is the most probable outcome when a predator is involved.

The call came in as I was driving through Dallas, Texas. Just twenty miles ahead, Dr. Jacobsen and his wife were missing their two-year-old Yorkshire terrier. I agreed to come right away, as I was nearby.

Upon my arrival I noticed a large home surrounded by trees. The home was beautifully set amid the heavily forested woods. There was no fence. The client notified me that they actually had their last sighting of their dog on a surveillance tape. She had scratched at the door to be let back in, but in the chaos of bringing home their newborn twins, no one had heard little Princess scratching at the back door.

Cade began the case for us. An air-scent dog, Cade took scent and immediately ran to the rear of the yard and tracked straight out into the woods. He stopped about a quarter mile from the physician's property. He alerted that this was the end of Princess's scent trail.

We walked back to the truck, knowing that it was not a good sign that the scent trail had just ended in the woods. I wanted another opinion, so I next brought out Twist. Twist took scent at the last spot Princess had been seen. The small Jack Russell tracking dog headed into the woods navigating a slightly different route than Cade, but she ended and alerted at the same place. She too had found that the scent ended in the middle of the woods.

It is important to us that we have as many opinions and noses on a case as we can, so next up was Dodger, our little professor and microscope. Our cadaver specialist, Dodger tracked into the woods using a completely different route. Unlike Cade and Twist, Dodger is a true ground tracker and follows the actual footsteps of the missing dog. He went only forty feet into the woods until he found tiny bits of fur on the forest floor and in the bushes. The small pieces of fur were almost impossible to see, but Dodger is an expert. A few more feet down the trail, Dodger alerted on blood. This was the point of impact where Princess had encountered a coyote and met her demise. Air-scent dogs Cade and Twist had headed out into the woods and followed the scent trail as the predator carried the body of the small dog away. They followed her scent trail until there was nothing left to follow and the small dog had been consumed.

The pet owner then told us that they could see on the tape that Princess had heard something and had then run to the bushes but had never come out. While watching the tape, we found that Princess had entered the bushes just twenty feet from where Dodger had found her fur. It is likely that the feisty Yorkie ran into the woods to play with the coyote as if it was another dog. This is a tactic coyotes use to lure a dog into their domain.

The pet owners were saddened at their family member's passing but thankful for the closure, as they had been combing the woods and had been unable to find anything.

It took the dog team to tell Princess's story.

Actions and Activities to Pursue

The following are the actions and activities suggested for this scenario. The techniques and actions suggested are described in detail in **Section 3: Actions, Activities, and Techniques.**

- **First-response protocol** in the first hours.
- **Ground-zero search** of home or point of escape.
- **Tiger Line Physical Search**: see the activity instructions, and be aware you are looking for evidence that is best seen within eighteen inches of the ground, basically knee level.
- **Witness development** near point of escape for sightings, information, and leads. Ask others if predators have been known to come into the area.
- **Check emergency animal hospitals** by phone.
- **Neighborhood grid search** for older dogs and all small dogs.
- **Check animal shelters**, humane societies, and so on.
- **Post Signage** for sightings and any information from the point of escape.
- **Create Flyers** to hand to people as a calling card when you are searching and developing witnesses and sightings.
- **Hire a professional with tracking dogs** if you feel your pet may have met this situation. Professionals with trained K9s are able to follow the pet's scent even if the pet has met with a predator and its body has been carried away. Although there are rarely any remains, a coyote leaves classic indicators, and experienced tracking dogs are well versed in following even if the pet is deceased. Many professionally trained K9s will continue to follow the scent until they are pulled up or there are no remains left to follow.

There are additional instructions and suggestions at http://www.howtofindalostdog.org/more-about-the-nine-scenarios.html.

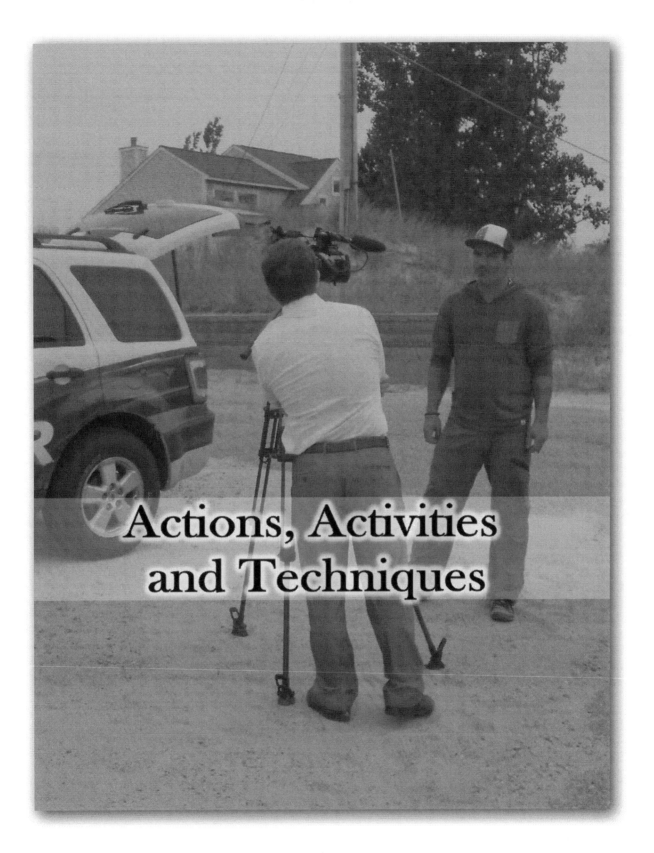

Actions, Activities
and Techniques

First-Response Protocol

If your dog has been missing longer than forty-eight hours, only scan this technique.
The situation may be brought on by a trip to the Veterinarian or a front door left open, but the worst of nightmares begins when a beloved four-pawed family member escapes or goes missing.

If you have never encountered this situation, the experience can be quite a shock. For many of us, it can be paralyzing at a time when we need to be on our best game. It is a time for action when you may feel the need to curl up and just cry.

Below is a list of the most immediate activities to pursue when first you realize your pet has escaped or is missing.

Relax and Don't Panic

But also don't wait to start looking. Statistics prove that pet owners with the greatest likelihood of recovering their dog start looking immediately and have an organized approach. Be one of these pet owners.

Ground-Zero Property Search

Make sure your pet is really missing. If you did not see him or her escape or do not know of anyone who did, take a few minutes to do a quick sweep of your property and the most obvious hiding spots before bolting for the front door to look. Check your home, yards, garage, outbuildings, under beds, and so on. Sick or injured animals hide much of the time.

Prepare to Search
What to bring

You can gather this in five minutes or less. A better idea is to have someone else do this while you do the ground-zero search.

- Photo of pet
- Twenty cards with twenty-four-hour phone number and the words "Lost Dog"
- Treats

- Leash
- Carrier (if dog is not leash trained or will respond and run to crate)
- Whistle, squeaky toy, or clicker if pet has been trained to one or thinks they are fun and will respond
- Box of high value or fragrant treats that you can rattle if pet responds to the sound

Immediately, grab a photo of your dog and a business card with your phone number on it. If you don't have a business card or if the card does not have a phone number on it that you will answer twenty-four hours a day, take a yellow sticky, index card, or any scrap of paper and write your cell-phone number on it with the words "Lost Dog." Make at least twenty. Don't forget the leash or carrier and treats in case bribery is necessary. There is something in your refrigerator that will work in an emergency. Hot dogs, last night's dinner, bologna, cheese, or even people cookies will work.

Bring in the Troops
This is the time to call in your friends, family, and neighbors. If possible, recruit those who will be supportive in your efforts and understand your concern and attachment for your dog. Call in your supportive friends and not the naysayers; you need to keep yourself focused in your efforts.

Make It Easy for the Dog to Return
Leave someone at the point of escape or your home in case your dog returns. If no one is available, leave a gate, car door, or crate open or something that the pet is familiar with and may want to stay near. A high value food or treat that your dog likes can also work. In the worst case and with nothing else to leave, take off a piece of your clothing and leave it at the front door, near the gate, or on the front porch.

Head for the Door!
Choose a direction
If you know in which direction the dog went, go that way (and forget the ground-zero search as you know he's out). If you are not sure of the direction, and your pet has done this before, go in the direction he went the last time he got out. If you have no idea whatsoever, go to the spot where you think the dog escaped and assume he went right. This is a percentage call, because dogs turn to the right more often than they turn to the left. If, however, there is something scary to the right or something is blocking the way, then choose another direction.

You Did Not See the Dog Go Missing, or the Dog Has Been Missing More Than an Hour
If you did not see the dog go missing or you think he or she has been gone more than an hour, then a driving search is best. Drive slowly and methodically, and scan in front, to the side, down cross streets and alleys, and out across fields and parks. The ideal situation is to have a driving team. One drives and

scans to the left while the passenger scans to the right and stops passersby with the photo and lost cards by asking, "Have you seen this dog?" Remember to leave the telephone card with everyone you ask.

If you drive for more than an hour with no sightings, return to the point of escape to figure out the direction of travel the fleeing pet went in. Knock on doors and talk to everyone outside. Ask anyone you see as you are searching out direction and sightings, "Have you seen this dog?" Show the picture and leave a phone-number card or sticky with them. If someone has seen your pet, go in the direction they direct you to and use the above protocols while continuing to gather sightings, evidence, and direction.

Follow your leads and sightings until you either find your pet or run out of clues and sightings. If you go over one hour with no sightings or clues, head back to the point of escape to update and design a more formal search strategy with public awareness, development of witnesses, and effective activities that will move your search forward.

Ground-Zero Search

If your dog has been missing longer than forty-eight hours, or you know he is off your property, skip this step.

This technique may appear to be an extra step, but in reality it can be a great time saver as well as a life saver. I have had numerous situations where a pet owner has called panicked only to find out within a day or two that the pet was still on his or her property.

I recommend that you do a uniform search of your house, garage, basement, barn, outbuildings, and property. The easiest method is to take each structure and go through it room by room in succession.

Always clear the room in one direction. Start in the same place in each room. As most people are right-handed, it is easier for most to clear the room from left to right. As you approach closets, cabinetry, furniture, and so on, thoroughly look in, under, behind, and inside of each high in closets and low in kitchen cabinets. Do not assume that a basement was never accessible to the pet and that it could not be in there. In the course we enter, exit, and pass through many rooms and situations that will never reg memory.

We have found a cat outside when the pet owner was absolutely sure that the ten out. She spent hundreds of dollars on different professionals coming to search perimeter of the house, inside the walls, and so on, only to find out through outdoor surveillance cameras (which she felt was a waste of time, but an expert convinced her otherwise) that the cat was in fact outside. She had forgotten that she empties the trash every night, and her brain did not create a unique memory of that night, so she had done that task without thinking - the cat had slipped out. In a sadder case, a pet owner's elderly dog had crawled under a piano and died. All search efforts were outside the house, and the dog was found on the fifth day deceased. Same with swimming pools: best to check the pool and the filtering system.

How to Call for Your Dog

One of the most difficult parts of the search is trying to remain calm. As you call your pet, it is important to use your inside, affectionate voice. When we are stressed or trying to project our voice, we put tension in our voice, which most pets perceive as something wrong. So if the pet is already skittish or may be afraid of reprimand, low, soft voices and affectionate clicks and noises you use regularly are much more effective than screaming his or her name at the top of your lungs. Most of us have funny, affectionate, or maybe even goofy pet names we call our beloved pets. As embarrassing as it is, this is the voice and words to use. It is quite a sight to see a big football player walking down the sidewalk, calling, "Pookie wookie, Daddy loves you." But it works! Explain it to the neighbors later. Find your pet now.

Call the pet's name but stop to listen. Call...listen (pause to a count of ten). Call...pause to a count of ten...listen. And so on.

Remember to use your indoor, happy, affectionate voice like you want to play or give affection. If you have trained your pet to a whistle, a squeaky toy, shaking a box of food or treats, or any other welcoming response, use this now.

Walk, ride, or drive? This will depend on your pet, the availability of help, and how long it has been since the pet escaped.

If the dog escapes and you notice within minutes: A scared, excited, or bolting dog with you hot on his heels is best caught on foot, and *don't* chase him. Try these steps.

If you see your dog, try these steps in this order:

- Run backward while facing the dog, and encourage him to follow with soothing words. If this is an escape artist, the words should encourage play. For shy dogs, a more soothing display of encouragement is best. If the dog does not respond...
- Drop to your knees and use your talking inside voice. If the dog stops running, encourage him with soothing voice, not anger, until he is within easy reach, and then calmly bring the dog into your control. If the dog does not respond...
- Pretend you're eating something yummy while on your knees. If the dog does not respond...

- Roll over onto your back with your face toward the sky, and continue to encourage the dog to approach. This is a sign of your submission and invitation. Many dogs instinctually respond to these cues. Put the treats on your chest and wait. If the dog runs or leaves…
- Develop a strategy to "head him off at the pass." Intersecting an animal's forward direction is better than flat-out sprinting behind. Angulation in the direction you think he or she will go is more effective. Once at the intercept point, begin the above steps.

How to Approach or, More Precisely, *Not* Approach the Roaming Dog

Scenario Specific: Roaming Dog

This is one of the toughest parts of this process and the hardest for many pet owners to understand. Your loving, bed-sharing dog *may not come* to you when called and may even bolt and run if she sees you.

This is so common as to be expected, so please do not take this personally or attach any deep meaning to her fear. Your dog is surviving by using her feral instincts, and in her suitcase of survival techniques is an extreme flight response that she needs in order to survive just like her wild cousins, the wolf and coyote. Running and bolting is a very canine response to the situation your dog is encountering.

I encourage you to read this and expect that she will run from you. Be prepared for this possibility with your own bag of feral tricks.

If you see your dog roaming at large, and your dog has been missing less than forty-eight hours and is not shy:

First try a play action *unless the dog is shy; then skip this step.* Run backward while facing the dog, and encourage him to follow with soothing words. If this is an escape artist, the words should encourage play. If dog does not respond within one minute…

Drop to your knees and use your talking inside voice. If the dog stops running, encourage him with a soothing voice until he is within easy reach, and then calmly bring the dog into your control. If your dog does not respond…

Pretend you're eating something yummy while on your knees. If the dog does not respond…

Roll over onto your back with your face toward the sky, and continue to encourage the dog to approach. This is a sign of your submission and invitation. Many dogs instinctually respond to these cues. Put the treats on your chest and wait…

If the dog runs off, do your best to watch where she goes, *but do not chase her.* We do not want the dog to feel pursued or hunted. Our ultimate goal is to capture her, but if she will not approach, then our next objective is to have her stay in the area so that attraction and possibly a capture process can begin.

If your dog has been missing more than forty-eight hours, please just trust me and use this technique:

Please assume she will not come to you as she normally would.

Do not look directly at your dog. Angle your body sideways in reference to the dog, and look at the ground to the dog's immediate left. Do not meet the dog's gaze, and do not respond if she appears to be confused. You are the calm in the storm; hold fast like a pier anchoring a ship to the shore. Remain steadfast regardless of how she behaves.

Try to control your anxiety, fear, and even joy at seeing her. Take a deep breath and even let out a sigh, which will calm you more than just the deep breath. Picture a calm scene as you prepare to drop to your knees. Let your shoulders drop and your hands hang loosely at your sides. Do not clench your fists or hold your breath. Your dog in her extremely sensitive and alert state may perceive any tension in your body as a sign that something is wrong.

Immediately but quietly drop to your knees, and use a quiet but affectionate inside voice. *Do not use any play-type encouragements or actions that encourage play.* If the dog stops and looks at you, stay on your knees and continue to encourage with a quiet, soothing voice. Use the dog's nickname and any loving phrases that encourage a calm behavior. If the dog does not approach within thirty seconds…

Pretend you're eating something yummy while on your knees. If the dog does not approach within sixty seconds…

Roll over onto your back with your face toward the sky and your belly up.

Stop talking and lie quietly. This position is a sign of your submission and invitation to the dog, who is now working off a feral instinct. Many dogs will instinctually respond to this cue. Put the treats on your chest and wait. Even if she initially runs off, stay on the ground. One pet owner stayed in this position for thirty minutes and another was on her back for two hours before their dogs decided to approach. Be patient; your dog needs to travel back to domesticity, and right now she is perched for flight at the edge of survival. She is ready to flee at the slightest provocation.

If the dog runs off, do your best to watch where he goes, but do not give chase. We do not want the dog to feel hunted or pursued. My recommendation is to get out a book, sit down, and quietly read out loud for the next hour. Make it a good book that you can become engrossed in. Keep your treats nearby, and if he comes back or pokes his head out, gently toss out a smelly treat and go back to reading until he will come near enough for you to bring him under your control.

How to get the dog under your control once she is near:

Do not ever lunge or make a fast move toward the dog. She is far quicker than you are.

Instead, offer her smelly food. I like hot dogs or cheese, but there are many options, which you can find in the section under "Attraction and Surveillance." Offer her *bite-size pieces* no bigger than the tip of your thumb with the hand that you are less adept with. For instance, if you are right-handed, offer with the left so you can use your right arm and hand to eventually bring her under control.

While hopefully still on your knees or in a prone position, gradually bring the treats closer to your body and then across your body so that your more adept arm can reach around her body or easily grasp her collar when she reaches for the treat. Use this rule of thumb: She must accept at least ten pieces of bite-sized treat before you even consider reaching for her and using the across-your-body capture technique. Be patient. Do not move fast. If she jumps back when you move to grasp her, nonchalantly continue to offer treats in this way. If she has come this far, she will eventually allow you to get her under your control.

If the dog does not return after she has seen you and you have staked yourself out reading or listening to music, it is likely she will need to be attracted in, conditioned, and captured with other means.

Do not be discouraged. Proceed to attraction, conditioning, surveillance, and capture. You have come this far; you can do this.

There are additional instructions and suggestions for this technique at http://www.howtofindalostdog.org/more-actions-and-techniques.html.

Notifying Emergency Animal Hospitals

In this technique I am specifically referring to emergency animal hospitals where a pet could be brought if it met with an accident after hours.

If your pet went missing at night, I **strongly suggest calling** all the emergency animal hospitals in your area by the next morning to see if anyone brought in a stray or injured animal matching your pet's description. You generally need to call very early, as many of these hospitals close by 8:00 a.m.

If a pet goes missing in the afternoon to early morning, a quick call to these hospitals is in order. If your pet is still missing after forty-eight hours, you can then decide if you or someone else would like to bring the emergency hospitals a flyer with your pet's picture on it.

First mode of action: *call* them.

Developing Leads and Witnesses

Although many people absolutely dread this part of the search, it can be the best way to develop leads so your search can expand and go to the next level. There are three times in your search that you may need to knock on doors or question people on the street. The first is near the point of escape immediately after you notice your pet has gone missing; the second is when you are developing witnesses and a possible direction or scenario of what may have happened; the third is when you are trying to determine if in fact your pet has been in a certain area after receiving a sighting or lead.

Knocking on Doors...Talking It Up

Door knocking should be done in the daylight with at least one other person. Do not approach fenced front yards that say "beware of dog," and use your strongest intuition about approaching residences. Do not go inside people's homes. If requested to enter, explain that you appreciate the offer but that you have many homes to cover in your search. With all that said, put on some comfortable shoes, take a deep breath, and try to enjoy with the expectation that you will learn a key piece of information every time you knock.

- Always keep someone informed about your location, and check in with them often.
- Always carry bait food, a leash, pen and paper, a cell phone, and anything else of necessity.
- A street map directs you to sighting areas quickly and without question.
- A flashlight allows you to look for hiding places under buildings or in small, dark spaces and holes.

- Dress appropriately for weather conditions. Be safe; don't venture alone into unfamiliar or dangerous territory.

Rule of thumb: It is generally not necessary to go more than ten houses in each direction of the point last seen when trying to confirm sightings. Do not spend six hours knocking on all the doors in a subdivision. You really only need to have conversations with people in an immediate area surrounding an important event or sighting in the search. Your signs are your extension of your efforts into the homes you cannot feasibly reach.

Note: Do not confuse this activity with a neighborhood grid search, which involves witness development as well as searching individual properties. Grid searches cover many more properties than basic witness development.

Door Knocking Script and Suggestions for Initiating Responses

The following is a suggested script and queries to be used when pursuing leads and sightings and developing witnesses for missing pets. Be creative and add your own questions, but be brief and do not accuse anyone or tell a long, drawn-out scenario that you think may have happened to your pet. This is not the time for "I think X stole my dog." Let the person you are questioning bring up his or her own information. If you *do* have something in particular to ask, ask about it in a *nonthreatening* way. Even if you suspect someone, don't go into a story about it. Ask leading questions that would lead you to believe you may be right. The most important strategy is to get the most out of each communication or party you talk with. Let them tell you what they noticed first; then Profiling Query them more in that direction.

I am a big proponent of knocking on a door instead of using the doorbell. It is probably just my little quirk, but it is what I do. As soon as you knock, take a big step back away from the door. This is nonthreatening and lets whoever comes to the door have space. If they look through a security peephole before opening the door, it gives them a view of your face and torso. I would also suggest smiling and holding up a flyer or photo of your pet. This lets them know that you are not on their doorstep to sell them something.

Note: *A pause is a count of 1-2-3-4-5. This pause gives the person's memory or subconscious time to not only access the memory but make the most out of the question too.*

When they answer the door, smile, introduce yourself, and ask:

"Hi, I am Jerry from down the street, and my dog is missing. Have you or anyone in your household seen this dog?" (Hold up the picture of your pet.)

Pause.

"He has been missing since _____."

Pause.

"He got out on Saturday [or whatever] and did not return [or explain the scenario in very brief form]."

Pause.

They have now had enough time to go back in their memory to the day or time thereabouts and come forward, sifting through their memory for recall.

The next question elicits a response for possible leads as to why your pet did not return.

"Are you aware of anything that may have happened on _____? Parties, guests, service people visiting your house, or anyone else that may have been in the neighborhood on that day?"

If you are concerned your pet was possibly rescued or taken, ask this question:

"Have you noticed anyone in the neighborhood that you feel may not live here or was possibly driving too slow or maybe even stopped and approached a dog?"

Add any questions of your own.

"Would you mind keeping this flyer in case you or someone in your household remembers something or you see him in the future?"

Thank them and move to the next house.

This question-and-answer stop should take about three to four minutes. Be friendly, sincere, and courteous. The goal is to have their eyes and ears working to help you.

If while you are knocking and gathering information, an individual has what appears to be credible information, write it down in your sightings journal using the format provided. If the information is substantial and changes the focus of your search, you need to stop, gather your thoughts, and alter your strategy, taking into account the new information.

An example of new information that you feel is credible is:

- Resident saw a car stop and pick up a small dog, and the description matches your pet.
- You have been puzzling over how your small dog got out when the gate was closed and have really thought that dog was taken from your yard. Resident states he or she saw your gate open and closed it for you, not realizing your dog had gotten out.
- Neighbor thought he or she heard an animal crying or whimpering like it had been injured around the time your pet went missing.

How to Handle Sightings

The sightings are the key to moving an investigation and search forward and to the next level. Most of the activities we pursue are performed to achieve sightings. It is important not to underestimate these calls, as they are important pieces to your puzzle. Handling them with accuracy and timeliness is very important.

The Sightings Journal Form or Sightings Query Form

As the calls and information come in, it is important to have some formal way in which to keep track. Slips of paper and backs of envelopes mysteriously disappear at exactly the time you need them. I strongly encourage the use of a notebook, either store bought or put together with the blank Sightings Journal form included in this book.

Do not underestimate the value of this activity. Print out ten copies of this form. It will help you keep track of where you have been, which sightings were valid, and which "go sees" were animals other than your own so you do not have to keep checking the same area for a similar animal that is not your pet.

Types of Calls
Sympathizers and supporters

You will be surprised at the number of calls you receive that have nothing to do with seeing your pet. Some will be support calls from others who understand the situation you are in, as they have been there themselves. Others may call just to see if you have found your pet. We call these "sympathizers and supporters," and in some cases these people have become important to our cases. I encourage you to note them in your Sightings Journal as sometimes they may offer to help, and you may need the help if the search is prolonged and extends.

"I think I saw your dog"

These are the calls we are waiting for. I like to distinguish which type of call I am dealing with at the very beginning of a conversation. At the very beginning of a call, and in your most polite and sincere voice, I encourage you to ask, "Have you seen him?" The polite and sincere can be tough if you have received twenty sighting calls that day, but remember, the caller has gone out of his or her way to call you, and for some it may be the first time they have extended this type of help. So be polite and enthusiastic and proceed to ask the questions from the Sightings Journal worksheet.

Although it is important to ask the questions necessary to find out if in fact they have seen your pet, it is equally important to allow the callers to tell their story.

Important: Do not prompt the callers with any physical descriptions of your pet. Allow them to describe the animal they saw. You may, however, ask if the pet had any characteristics that were unusual or stood out. It is important to fill out the Identifying Characteristics and Profile in the "Search Management" section and keep it available by the phone at all times.

When the caller describes the location, have him or her be very specific. For example, your location might look something like this:

Street: *On Lamar Drive.* **Cross Street:** *Blaney right where Lamar ends.*
Near: *The gate to the creek closest to the tan house with cactus. Traveling toward Somerset Drive.*

Dog was trotting with tail up, sniffing around

By the description, it would be very easy to find this location and to also gain information about how this pet is feeling. A dog trotting with tail up and stopping to sniff is not experiencing extreme fright or in a panicked state. He is more likely on walkabout and maybe enjoying himself at that moment. Fears that the dog may be bolting in a state of fear could be alleviated with this sighting. Dogs bolting or running blindly are more likely to meet with an accident as they are not thinking clearly, so this sighting can give a pet owner a little peace of mind, as the pet appears to be in a calm state.

"I am looking at your dog right now"

If you receive this call, in your most enthusiastic and sincere voice, ask the caller to please stay and watch your pet, as you are already out the door and getting in the car. If you can keep the caller on the phone and converse about the dog he or she is looking at, the caller can monitor the animal should it move from the location. If the dog begins to move, the caller can tell you in which direction and where.

Sometimes it is helpful to ask the caller to try and call the animal by using the pet's name and see what the response is. However, rule of thumb:

If your dog has been gone longer than forty-eight hours, it is usually better to ask the individual to not approach or attempt to catch her.

We have on more than one occasion experienced an enthusiastic caller accidentally chasing the pet into the street. So encourage the caller to stay with you on the phone. Sometimes that may not be easy. We have had callers say, "I see your dog right now, but I am on my way to church, and I don't want to be late." In one case, the client was just four minutes away and had been trying to get close to her dog for over six weeks! The caller hung up, refusing to stay another few minutes. The dog had left by the time its owner arrived, and the pet owner had no idea in which direction he went.

So continue to talk with the caller and try to persuade him or her to stay until you arrive. Remind the caller of the reward, how important your pet is to you, how you have been unable to sleep—use anything, but try to convince the caller to stay and watch the pet as you frantically but calmly try to get to the location. Most callers will stay until you arrive. Remember to say thank you, even if it is not your pet when you arrive.

Going to See—the "Go Sees": Checking and Confirming Sightings

This phrase was given to me by a client, and she aptly named this part of the search. After hanging up with the caller, you must now decide if this sounds like a valid lead and sighting of your pet. Try not to judge the callers, their sincerity, or if you like them. Look only at the information they provided and decide if it matches your characteristics and how you know your pet. This decision must be made rather quickly, as you should get to the location to see if you can locate the animal the caller is reporting to you. Even if the caller's sighting was three days ago, you still need to go check it out unless you have a more recent confirmed sighting. This is all about timing and locations.

Drive or walk, whichever is quicker, to the area of the sighting. Once you get within six or seven blocks of the possible sighting, begin to look right and left, scanning yards, down cross streets, and alleys in case your pet is now traveling toward you. I have had people race to sightings and then pass their dog on the way because they were focused on the location, not the scan.

If the sighting was within two hours of your arrival, I suggest you drive around first. I recommend that you spiral out from the location going in the direction the caller said your pet was traveling. When in doubt of the direction, remember dogs turn to the right more than left, and if a corner looks inviting, a dog may just keep sniffing his way along the yards without crossing the street. Now, this rule of thumb is not set in stone. When we are tracking a dog at large who is doing the "sniff and pee" routine, we generally track in large spirals and go up one street and then down the next. It can be very haphazard, and catching up can be very difficult, but it is highly likely. The pet owners who recover their pets are those who are persistent, diligent, and creative.

If the sighting appears to be valid, but after an hour you have not seen your dog, go back to the sighting location, get out, and put up signs. *When in doubt, place signs.*

You should also knock on doors while you are in the area and see if anyone else saw the pet and the direction it went. More than once, a pet owner has proceeded to knock on doors and come upon a dog that looked like his. Realizing the dog looked similar, the pet owner asked if the pet had been out recently, and the owner confirmed that the dog had in fact just gotten back from a jaunt. This dog was most likely the one which the caller saw. If you find the pet in question and it is not your pet, move on. There is no need to post signs *if you are sure* you have found the animal the caller reported.

As you are looking for your pet, don't be surprised if you find other people's missing pets. A large number of our clients find someone else's dog and are able to return the pet. One client found six missing dogs, while another found twelve. They were able to find the owners for most of the dogs. The remainder of the dogs were put up for adoption after an extensive search for their families.

Don't get discouraged because there are not enough calls or too many calls. Note each sighting and lead, as each can be very important as the search unfolds. Should you decide to bring in professional help or scent-specific tracking dogs, the sightings and leads are key to moving the search forward.

Google Earth

If you are not familiar with this aerial computer program, now is a good time to learn it. It is a free download from Google and is very easy to use. We use this program extensively to map sightings, grid neighborhoods, and develop the search-and-recovery strategy. This is a great tool to keep track of location and sightings information.

There are additional instructions and suggestions for this technique at http://www.howtofindalost-dog.org/more-actions-and-techniques.html.

Make the most of yo

The Call & Sight

Type of call: Sighting	
Lead Supporter Other	Date called:
Name of caller/witness:	Phone N

Pet Identification Lineup Card

Probing questions to ask to confirm identity of t'

1. To compare size:
If you were standing next to the animal you saw, where on you
What would you guess the animal you saw weighed? More than 10 pou..

2. Unique features
Did you notice a collar? *(Do not state whether your pet did or did not have a collar on when she we..*
Did you notice _____ (a unique or prominent feature your pet has like tail, ears,color)
Can you describe the color or markings of the animal you saw?

Information about the sighting or lead

Where did you see my pet?	Street and cross street	Near/Landmark
When did you see my pet?	What time of day? Was it dark or light outside?	
If my dog ran off, in which direction did he go?	What was my dog doing when you her/him? walking trotting resting eating other	

Doing the Go See's... The Results from the sighting

Went to check lead or sighting on:	Comments and Information for future reference:

This is a technique I adapted from the law-enforcement arena. The purpose of the card is to establish a confirmed sighting of your dog. When callers or witnesses notify you that they believe they have seen your pet, it is important to remember that in most cases they have seen the animal only briefly and are trying to recreate the memory with the help of a photo they have seen of the pet. The callers want to help you and genuinely want this to be your pet so that they can rejoice in your happy ending. It is important to have a way to verify that the dog the caller saw was in fact your pet.

Designing the Lineup

It is best to use a format with the photos of at least six different dogs on it. One of the photos will be your pet, but that photo on the card should not be the same photo that is on your signs or flyers. The photo you use on the lineup may even be from a different angle or side.

When designing a lineup card, we generally go to the Internet to find pets that are of a similar color and size to the dog we are looking for. Many of us go to Google Images and use key words that most closely describe the breed, color, type, or look of the missing dog. Your card need not be fancy, and you will not need many of these cards, as you will not leave them with people. They are for confirmation and identification purposes only.

You can copy and paste the different photos to a Word document or other graphics program. Once completed, you can print it out or turn it into a .jpg or .pdf document so it can be presented to witnesses either in person or by e-mail.

Using the Lineup

The goal is to show the card to witnesses and people who believe they have seen your pet. You simply show them the card and ask them which animal on the card most closely resembles the animal they saw. Do not give hints or encouragement as to which pet is yours. As much as possible, you are trying to confirm a sighting, and although we appreciate all input and help, it is important to try and confirm that it really was your dog the witness saw.

So ask: **"Which of the animals on this card most closely resembles the animal you saw?"**

Take the new information, and if the sighting appears to be confirmed, move your search to the new area and begin looking for the animal the caller or witness saw. If you do not find the animal, create awareness in the area with signage.

Making the Rounds: Checking with Animal Shelters, Humane Societies, Animal Control, and Other Public Agencies

Do not wait on this. Some pets are picked up by animal control or turned in by well-meaning citizens right away.

If your pet is missing in the morning, it is possible that the pet was picked up by the animal-control truck and will not go back to the shelter until late afternoon. Unless you *know for sure* your pet is on the truck, it is a waste of your valuable search time to wait at the shelter when you could be doing other productive search-related activities.

Below is a brief explanation of the differences in animal-welfare groups. Depending on where you live, your area may have all of them or none of them.

You need to visit them all. Do not rely on their Internet postings or information over the phone or the fact that you have left them a flyer. There are so many stories where the pet was at the shelter and the pet owner was told it was not—my own dog included. *Go in person* and check every square foot of the place they will allow. Twenty-three years ago, I managed one of the largest humane societies in the country, and I can tell you that puppies were sometimes put in with kittens, injured dogs were in with biters, and old dogs were in the cat room. Even special strays that a staff member might like can be put

in an area other than strays. You get my gist. *Go look everywhere in the building they will allow!*

Animal-Control Agencies

These are county or city agencies responsible for enforcing animal regulations and control. Some agencies will have officers and trucks that pick up strays and accept owner and stray surrenders. They usually have strict requirements and hours. The fact is that the large stray populations are community and public health problems, not the bad or evil intent of the employees of these agencies. In some cases the agencies may have euthanasia policies for pets that have been unclaimed in the facility longer than three days. Do not rely on the fact that your pet is micro-chipped. Although microchips are a great invention, their use has not caught up with their marketing. Do not leave your pet's life to the discretion of a microchip that may have moved or a staff member in a hurry who scans quickly or ineffectively. Contrary to popular belief, all shelters and agencies do not scan for a chip.

Animal Shelters

These agencies can be private or municipal, and their scope and effectiveness are determined by their funding and ability to staff. They typically house stray, abused, rescued, or owner-surrendered animals, but check with the city or county where your pet went missing. Some areas may have only one, while others have more than one. In some places, several communities may share one facility. You need to find out what you are dealing with in that area and where the next shelter's boundaries are. I know of one area in Texas where the boundaries of three different shelters are within six blocks of each other. Most pets can travel that distance easily.

Humane Societies

Most of these are private or not-for-profit, and they can work in conjunction with animal shelters and animal control. In some areas they are all housed together in the same place, and a citizen may not even be able to tell which is which. On a national scale, they work for the welfare of all animals, but the large organization does not generally work closely with the individual private organizations bearing their name.

Rescue Groups

These are the citizens and individuals who take in animals and rescue them. From purebreds to mutts, cougars to crows, there is a rescue group for just about everything in the large metropolitan areas of the United States. Your challenge is trying to uncover who is who. If you have a purebred dog that is easily identifiable by its breed, you should inquire if there is a rescue group for that breed. Many concerned citizens would rather turn in a stray to a rescue group than to a shelter, because they fear the animal they have saved may ultimately be euthanized if the owner does not claim it. Their fears are valid in many cases. Unfortunately, the animal shelters or humane societies may be the only centralized notification center in an area. If a pet has gone missing and is given to a rescue group, the pet owner may have no way of finding it if the rescue does not register the pet as missing with an agency.

Recently a large rescue network came under fire for providing a sort of Underground Railroad for rescued pets that stretched across several states. Pets that went missing in Los Angeles, California, could be transported as far away as Reno, Nevada, to be fostered while a suitable home was found. Unfortunately, the pet owners in Los Angeles had no way of knowing that their pet was in Reno and no way to get the information.

That said, I have great respect for those who do rescue and foster animals. It would be beneficial if there was one nationwide central clearinghouse where everyone could go to find a list of all pets lost and found in the country.

Dead-Animal Retrieval or Pickup Service

Although this is not the scenario you hope for, it is reality. Some pets do not return home because they have met with an accident that has caused their death. You will need to contact your local animal control or county waste management to find how this is handled. In some cases it will be a private company hired by the county; in others it will be crews hired specifically for this purpose, while others may have a sanitation-management company do it. Call to inquire what is used in the area where your pet disappeared. Call the agency and inquire if they keep records of the animals they pick up. You also need to ask if they will allow you to go through the records or if they have a staff member who can check to see if any of the deceased animals brought in match your pet's description and possible area. There are as many protocols in this area as there are companies, so you need to find out what is done in the area where your pet went missing.

Community-Awareness Campaign: Taking It to the Streets

Other people's eyes and ears
Signage

Most people are initially surprised when I tell them that signage is by far the most successful and productive activity we recommend. Some respond with "Yeah, I already did that." What they already did was use 8½ × 11 *flyers* and then tape or staple them all over the place or put them in mailboxes. This, however, is too limiting for a widespread campaign and search.

When deciding on how your energy is best used, I recommend this technique be at the top of your list. Experience has proven that if a pet owner places visible signage within the focused search area effectively, sightings and information from witnesses will generally begin to come in.

Ninety percent of pets recovered are returned due to other people's eyes or ears. The more people who know your dog is missing, the more witnesses there are to report sightings and information. It is a simple equation.

The following will describe the techniques I recommend. Be aware, this activity involves more than just taping a piece of paper with scribbled information in black marking pen on a pole.

If you want to increase your recovery chances tenfold, *do this activity and do it well.*

The Best Sign Option: Professional Waterproof Signage

After fourteen years doing this work, I have found that professionally produced eleven-by-seventeen laminated signs are the best. This is the format and imaging we use in our Home by Phone K9 Profiling sessions as well as our on location work.

During your search it is critical to use your time and energy effectively. When working with our pet owners, we strive to prioritize their actions. Making posters is time consuming while having them produced by commercial copy outlet is quick and effective. The costs for producing these can be higher than the Do-It-Yourself method but the time saved is generally worth it. As we order thousands of these signs every week, our company receives substantial discounts which we pass on to our clients.

Do-It-Yourself Poster

This is the least expensive effective sign method. It is best done with an assembly-line effort, as you will need to do a minimum of forty depending on your area and how the main thoroughfare streets surround your dog's point last seen.

Sign shopping list

1. *Minimum* twenty sheets of fluorescent poster board (they will be cut in half, so you will get forty). My personal favorite is fluorescent-pink sign board.
2. Two rolls of scotch double-back tape
3. One package of fluorescent 8½ × 11 paper
4. One permanent marker
5. One heavy-duty staple gun (not a paper or desk stapler; can be found in the hardware area of most "big box stores" or home improvement stores (about $24.00 to $39.00)

6. Two packages of zip ties at least twelve inches long (can be found in the automotive section of Walmart)
7. One package of plastic page protectors, if raining or excessively humid.

Making the signs—what do they say?
Think obnoxious billboard and visibility.

This cheap poster format is easy to do and can be duplicated in bulk. If possible, it is best to have at least one other person who can help you do this in an assembly-line fashion.

I have included an example of what the sign should look like when it is completed at the end of this section. Below is a written summary.

1. Buy large poster board from office supply or big-box retailer. Cut the sign board in half so that its size is approximately fourteen by twenty-two inches. Each piece of large poster board will make two signs.
2. You will be making two *flyers*, which you will eventually tape to the sign board.
   a. Flyer #1: Go to your computer and enlarge your pet's photo so that his body, head, and so on take up most of an 8½ × 11 (flyer size) sheet of paper. Most important is that from a distance of thirty feet, the pet's body and markings can be easily seen. A photo taken from the side is best. Print this out on white paper.
   b. Flyer #2: Go to Microsoft Word or a similar program to make this flyer. Use a contrasting fluorescent paper when you print it out. Set the page layout to the Landscape mode.
   - <u>First line</u> in font size 72. **LOST DOG**. Must be very visible.
     Optional: Most people in our culture can figure out the pet in the picture is the pet that is missing, so I am not big on descriptions here. But some pet owners feel a description is necessary, so if you must, place it below the above statement in smaller letters.
   - <u>Second line</u> in font size 36 to 48. **Emotional Impact Statement**—make them cry or at least go ah! Pet owners have used one of the following phrases depending on the situation and have also made their own statements up. Here are some of my suggestions:
     Distressed child…Please help!
     Senior citizen's pet…Please help!
     Disabled person's pet
     Therapy assistance dog
     Devastated family…Please help!
     Please help me find my best friend.
     Can't sleep! Can't eat! Help us find Gizmo.

This line should be in the middle of the flyer and clearly visible. Unfortunately, heartbroken family or adult no longer really works, so be descriptive and reach from your gut. If the pet is on meds, say so. The whole point is to create a reaction that will become tied psychologically to the memory of the photo. We need people to remember in case they see or hear about the pet in the future.

- <u>Third line</u>: It is important is to get others to know that you need any information or possible sightings.

  Please call with ANY information or if you have seen him.

  PLEASE DO NOT CHASE!

- <u>Fourth line</u>: Use one phone number here, and it is best if this is a phone you have with you twenty-four hours a day and seven days a week. Most pet owners use a cell-phone number. This like the first line should be in 72 font size.

  866-251-1599

  If you do not have a phone that you can carry with you or if you cannot answer your cell phone while you are at work, make sure your voice mail reflects that you are looking for your pet and that you will call people back immediately if they will leave their number.

- <u>Fifth line</u>: This line is expected in this day and age, and it needs to be on the sign.

  REWARD

  My experience and preference: I do not want substantial rewards on roaming dogs. Most people are not motivated to go out and look for a pet because of the dollar amount, and that is fine with me in the case of a roaming dog. I do not want anyone to try and catch a shy and skittish dog that has been on the roam for more than forty-eight hours or one that the pet owner knows is afraid of strangers.

   c. If you live in a bilingual area or have a bilingual neighborhood close by, I recommend doing the sign in two languages or at least certain lines. The Spanish phrase for "lost dog" is *perro perdido*, and the word for "reward" is *recompensa*. You will need to ask a translator for other languages or go online for a translation website in the language you need.

   d. Print both flyers out on their recommended paper colors.

3. You now have two flyers, and they need to be taped with scotch double-backed tape to one piece of your sign board.

   Place the poster board in a vertical position, take flyer #1 with the pet's photo, and place it at the top of the sign board, but leave **a border of pink or contrast around it.**

   Take flyer #2 printed **on your contrasting fluorescent paper**, and tape it with the double-backed tape below the photo flyer. Leave border in between the two flyers and **a border of pink at the bottom**.

   With black felt pen on the bottom pink border of the sign board, write:

   Please leave this up. Will remove by _____.

Pick a date that is ten to fourteen days out. We have better luck with a removal date in certain communities where signs are either not legal or are frowned upon.

4. You now have your first poster made. Duplicate this process by twenty to one hundred, and you will then be ready for the next step: using the posters effectively.

5. The setup and assembly time for twenty to thirty signs is about two hours.

How and Where to Place Your Signs

Now that you have your signs, you are ready to use them and get the phone ringing. First things first...

1. Go to your Google Earth map, and look at the point of escape or the point last seen. Spiral out and look in each of the eight compass directions. You are looking for high-traffic areas where people will be going to and from the grocery store or to and from work or school, thoroughfares that are the basic means of travel in the area that your pet went missing. Pick at least six to ten of these types of streets where you feel your signs will get the best drive-by traffic.

2. Once you have your streets, gather your hanging supplies that are listed on the shopping list and head for the car, hopefully with a friend or family member who can drive so you can staple or zip-tie depending on the situation.

Note: Be flexible with your street selection at this point. While driving you may see some other street that looks more easily accessible.

Hanging the Signs

Wooden poles and stakes are the easiest materials to hang your signs on. Please be aware that it may be illegal in your city or township to place signs or posters in public areas. Many people never check and just forge ahead, opting to find out if someone from public maintenance calls to tell them. Either way, I am making you aware that signage is frowned upon in some communities. That said, most pet owners go ahead realizing it is the best chance they have of recovering their pet. I do not know of anyone who has ever been fined, but I do know of cities that have crews that go out and take down signs almost as quick as they are put up. Should there be a problem, it is best to call the individual in charge of the public agency, explain your situation, and request that you be allowed to leave your signs up for a set number of days. Most cities will work with you on this as long as you agree to work within their parameters and time lines.

Convenience and grocery stores, banks, schools, parks, and the like

These are secondary locations for public awareness. Of this list my favorite is the convenience stores, as most people stop in at some time. Ask permission, or you may find that the sign is ripped down as soon as you leave. In some cases the next activity may be better for this type of post (flyers).

Important: You must check your signs regularly. If they are falling down or being torn down, you must replace them and look into the reason they are coming down.

There are additional instructions, suggestions, and information on how to get professional and effective signage quickly at http://www.howtofindalostdog.org/more-about-community-awareness.html.

Automated Mass-Calling Systems

Think Amber Alert for Lost Pets

Perhaps one of the most aggressive marketing campaigns for owners with missing dogs is the mass telemarketing-announcement industry or what I call Robo-Call systems. Many of these companies are legitimate and really do have a system in place that makes the calls to everyone within a given area; some, however, are scams.

An automatic mass-calling system is generally Internet based. The company will make several hundred to several thousand automated calls to the area surrounding the place where your dog went missing or was last seen. The calls are usually a canned speech with specific information about your dog broadcast to residential phone numbers.

The effectiveness of this service is good when combined with other community-awareness techniques. The most productive results for this technique are when a dog has been recovered by a local citizen within the calling area of the broadcast.

When a dog is roaming, it is best to use a custom announcement explaining that the dog is wandering or roaming the area and that the pet owner requests a call if the dog is seen. This will work best when a sign campaign is already in place, allowing the witness easy access to the phone number when the need arises.

There are some companies that are a scam. Many pet owners have called complaining that they gave their credit card to a company and then never had one call go out. This has happened many times and has even been featured on local news stations. The company will quote one fee and then bill the pet owner's credit card for more than they quoted. If a company contacts you and offers to do mass calling for any fee, I would be very careful. Go to the website for a list of companies we work with and consider to be professional and legitimate.

There are additional instructions and suggestions for this technique at http://www.howtofindalost-dog.org/more-about-community-awareness.html.

Car Signs

Car signs get your message out to the many as you drive.

The car signs we use are quick to produce and always have the photo of the dog as the centerpiece. Many dogs have been found as a result of this technique, including a dog lost in the woods who was seen by a hiker deep in the backcountry. The hiker was sitting at a stoplight when he saw the sign on the pet owner's car. In another case, a rescuer saw a car sign on a volunteer's car and knew that another rescue had just gotten the dog in as a stray and was about to put him up for adoption.

When the city or county absolutely forbids signs, posters, or flyers, this technique can be a lifesaver.

Car signs have been a relief for pet owners in cities where signs are absolutely, unequivocally not allowed. I have to say placing signs on vehicles does create a buzz. Clients who have tried this remark about horns honking and the thumbs-up they receive as they drive. Bottom line, the more people who know your pet is missing, the better your chances are of recovery. So put those photos and signs wherever you think they will get noticed.

How about T-shirts and jacket backs with a photo that says, "Have you seen Ernie? We miss him dearly!" It worked; he's home.

There are additional instructions and suggestions for this technique at http://www.howtofindalost-dog.org/more-about-community-awareness.html.

Flyers

The Ultimate Calling Card
Signs are to post; flyers are to give to people.

Your flyers are the calling cards that you leave with people. You can post them in secondary places, like gas stations, stores, and restaurants, where a large sign might be unwelcome, but for the most part they are to leave with people.

Flyers have more information than a sign or poster. There is generally a stronger call to action as well as a dynamic emotional impact statement. The description and history of the dog may also be more detailed.

We use flyers extensively in our investigations when we are knocking on doors or developing witnesses. We do not post flyers on the streets as the photos are not large enough to see or to create the impact we need on the streets. In many instances, we ask people to put them in their vehicle for easy access by using the power of suggestion. It can be effective to ask, "Can you save this flyer and carry it on your dashboard in case you see my dog?"

This is the inexpensive calling card you leave with people so they have your phone number and a reminder of your dog's missing situation.

There are additional instructions and suggestions for this technique at http://www.howtofindalost-dog.org/more-about-community-awareness.html.

LOST DOG

Very SHY Chihuahua
Brown/White—Male

R E W A R D

Rebel is a small brown and white neutered male Chihuahua. He is over 14 years old and is partially blind and has low level hearing.

He went missing from this neighborhood after getting out the gate in the nearby mobile home park.

He is a much loved pet and his owners are very anxious to get him back. Please call the number on this flyer immediately if you have seen him or see him in the future.

Rebel is my parent's dog and they are devastated . Please help us!

SAVE & CALL!

24/7 phone number: *888-569-5775*

Please call immediately if you or anyone in your household, think you may have seen him.

A heartbroken family is awaiting his return.

Place an Ad in the Local Newspaper

This is usually effective for a dog that has been recovered by a Good Samaritan. It generally produces very little results in the roaming-dog scenario.

Depending on the readership in your area, this can be an expected activity. With the increased use of the Internet, many people have stopped their subscriptions to the daily delivered newspaper, but their Internet presence may be increased.

Many media outlets have opted to put their classifieds and announcements, like Lost and Founds, online for the general public to read, which increases your scope. Many pets are still returned in this way, but it is much more hit-and-miss. Although I recommend you to post, I don't recommend you to rely on this activity solely. Remember to use the concepts in the flyer text when you design your ad. Be descriptive.

Examples

He's just a little guy...

We Love & Miss Him!

Missing 4/13 from Ragsdale Heights near Rodeo Dr.

Possibly picked up by concerned citizen.

Please HELP!

Senior Citizen's Companion
888-569-5775
$$ REWARD $$

General

    LOST Black and tan German shepherd, last seen 21st & Harvard, Shy 24/7 123-555-1212

For pet possibly rescued

    Missing near the Southgate mall and seen traveling west. Small black & tan dog—Yorks Very friendly. We love her too. REWARD and Our prayers answered.

    Please call 24/7 123- 555-1212

Looking for info with point last seen

    Large white dog last seen at Pembroke/Washington on 8/5 app. 3:00.

    Possibly hit by car. Please call 24/7 with any info. 123-555-1212

Roaming dog at large

    Red terrier cross with bristly face, seen at Red Grove Park but could now be anywhere. Any sightings, info, or thoughts welcome. Very upset child waiting for him to return call 123-645-2567

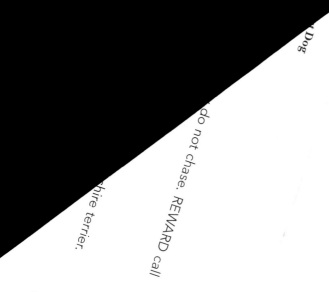

Prior ...   ...le most widely used lost-and-found protocols. With the increased
use of Facebook,   ...er social media sites, the use of websites has decreased.
    Many pet owners do p...   ...tional sites that offer state searches; however, the best solution is to
find the local lost-and-found sites that are used by citizens in the local area. Below is the keyword search
for this activity.
    Go to Google:
    Keyword search:
    Missing dog + (with your city, state or area)
    Lost dog + (with your city, state or area)
    Lost and found + (with your city, state or area)

    Below are websites that are national in scope:
    www.lostmydoggie.com
    www.petharbor.com
    www.craigslist.org
    www.petfinder.com
    www.dogdetective.com
    www.fidofinder.com
    www.lostandfound.com
    www.thecenterforlostpets.com
    www.findfido.com
    www.missingpet.net
    www.lostdogsdatabase.com
    www.pmia.com
    www.lostpetsos.com
    www.lostpaws.com
    www.homeagainid.com

Creating a Buzz with Social Media

Sightings and leads reported through social media are now a fact of life.
As people continue to incorporate social media into their everyday lives, this format of information and lead delivery makes up a large percentage of the information received by pet owners. Facebook has increased the volume of potential witnesses and has also through Lost Dog Community pages increased the number of people and volunteers who may get involved with a missing-dog search. In some cases, it has been because of a dog's Facebook community that the dog has been found and recovered.

When receiving potential leads from social media and e-mail, it is crucial to still incorporate all of your lead-confirming protocols to ascertain that the dog the witness is posting about is in fact your missing dog. Perhaps in no other format is it more likely that a witness can actually take a photo with his or her phone in real time and post the photos of the dog he or she believes may be your lost dog, instantaneously.

So ask the questions from your Sightings Profiling Query Form, and if at all possible, ask the original social media poster if you can talk by phone to clarify a few facts.

Most people are more than happy to talk with you. If they do not want to talk, record their information clarifying as much as possible. You can then make a decision as to the information's quality and validity. More than once a pet owner has gone out to a sighting only to find that the address did not exist or that the lead was in fact from a spammer who was invading the Facebook page.

You need to be careful with the information you are receiving, and you want to be safe always.

Facebook Pages, Groups, and Causes

In our work we use Facebook extensively. All cases we work are posted on Facebook and then shared to multiple pages and groups. In many instances, a page is created for the individual dog to better share and get his information out through social media users, who now number in the billions.

What is a profile?

A profile page is where all interactions with Facebook begin. You must have a profile, which is available for free with an e-mail address. The Facebook home page will have an area where you can sign up. This is true with Instagram and Twitter also.

What is a page?

A page is also free, and you can create a page for a business, cause, or otherwise by accessing this from your Facebook profile page. It can be a page that is used to brand and publicize the plight of a dog missing. Many pet owners set up a page to create awareness of their dog's missing situation to encourage shares and other interactions.

What is a group?

Groups are also free and are also accessed from your profile page. We use groups as posting tools, preferring to use groups created by others for the specific purpose of increasing awareness for the recovery of missing pets. Some individuals create groups for a specific missing dog, but we have not found this to be effective, as you must join a group as opposed to a page where you can readily see all the information.

We do, however, post our client's missing dogs to established groups with active members.

There are additional instructions and suggestions for this technique at http://www.howtofindalostdog.org/more-about-community-awareness.html.

Involving the Media

***T**his is ranked at the top in bringing awareness to your missing-pet situation.* Unfortunately, it can be difficult to get unless there is something unique about your pet, his life, your life, his position in your life (like therapy assistance or that he saved your child from drowning), or something you are doing that is unique to find him.

We have had media coverage for a missing pet because of the large reward offered, another time because an engaged couple was using the money they had set aside for their wedding to finance their search, but the majority of the time, our pet owners obtain media coverage because they have hired a nationally recognized pet detective with a tracking-dog team.

Whenever feasible, we encourage the use of the media. Although it can be time-consuming, nothing escalates awareness better than having a missing dog's picture on the six o'clock news. Recently, one of our cases was covered by FOX and NBC on the five, six, and ten o'clock news as well as the front page of the local newspaper. The pet owner was overwhelmed with calls, which are exhausting, but when you are trying to catch up with a dog roaming at large, it is welcome and necessary.

If you can get media coverage or you know someone who knows someone, by all means work this angle. Create a unique story line that has community interest before you call. Our clients have had the best luck when they present the story angle in its entirety to the news stations and the news team need only show up. Call all the local stations. Things happen, and you never know which station may need to fill a slot or who might need to cancel at the last minute.

When the reporters arrive to cover our searches, we make a deal: I will do the interviews and wear the mikes and so on if they will assure me that the missing pet's photo or sign and phone number will air on the screen for at least a few seconds. They generally will agree, however be aware that the news reporter or camera person does not edit and control the content. It never hurts to ask, however!

The media brings your pet's missing situation into everyone's home.

There are additional instructions and suggestions for this technique at http://www.howtofindalost-dog.org/more-about-community-awareness.html.

Press Release: For Immediate Release

Renowned Private Investigator and Tracking Dog Team
Called in to Search for El Reno Family's Much Loved Pet.

Brady is missing.

On December 9th, Brady, a much loved Miniature Schnauzer went missing from his home in El Reno. The family's search for their missing dog has been relentless. They have used social media, placed fliers and signs, used robo call amber alerts and have organized large community search parties. In the first weeks, sightings of Brady came in as the family scrambled to catch up with the frightened little dog.

Not knowing what else to do and refusing to give up, the family made the call to Karin TarQwyn the renowned Private Investigator. (www.k9pi.com)

TarQwyn's crack team of K9 Detectives, use their expertise and specially trained noses to locate missing dogs. With the highest success rate in the country, TarQwyn is the *go to detective* when a much loved pet goes missing.

(www.k9pi.com/dogteam_intropage.html)

The Search for Brady. Your crew and journalists are invited to participate and cover the campaign and investigation to find the beloved dog. Your participation will make a difference in the lives of these deserving citizens.

TarQwyn and her team will be on location in El Reno to begin the search for Brady on Tuesday morning.

About Karin TarQwyn: Karin TarQwyn and her K9 trackers are regularly featured in the media. They have appeared on PBS Animal Attractions, Animal Planet, The Today show, CNN, in People as well as over 50 newscasts and special features across the U.S.

TarQwyn and her tracking dogs always create high community and viewer interest when featured in a newscast. The team is frequently asked to participate in features for network sweeps weeks due to the high community interest generated by stories about her and the specially trained dog team.

TarQwyn appears as a LOST dog subject matter expert on the Animal Planet web site as well as that of the Dog Whisperer, Cesar Milan.

Additional media can be found here: http://www.k9pi.com/media.html

NOTE: Family members and volunteers as well as TarQwyn and her dogs, will be on location and available for interviews as they search for Brady.

For further information on locations and timing, contact 000-000-0000

email:

For case related questions, P.I. Karin TarQwyn can be reached at

Investigative Field Techniques

Spotlighting

This technique can also be used to locate an injured, elderly, ill, or hiding dog.

Spotlighting must be done in the dark. It is easier to see objects in the light of a spotlight than it can be in broad daylight, but you must have the right equipment. A flashlight is not very effective, so I do not recommend the use of even a high-powered one.

We use what I call a hunter's spotlight. They are available online and at most large retail sporting-goods stores. They run anywhere from $29.95 and up depending on the candle strength. You only need a bright spotlight, not one with radios, alarms, or reflector covers. We use spotlights with over two million candle power. Please note that most spotlights have to be plugged in for a minimum of four hours before they can be used, so plan accordingly.

How to use the spotlight

After charging, test to make sure you have a clear, unobstructed, bright light. Do not look into the lens, and remember that most spotlights tend to lose their charge quickly, some within twenty minutes, so do not waste any of the battery.

Your goal is to scan with the spotlight and see the pet's eyes reflect back to you as red dots in the dark. Shine the light under every bush, into every dark hiding spot, under houses, under decks, in sheds or pool houses, and anywhere you feel your dog may fit. Dogs who retreat and hide can fit in the smallest of spaces. You are looking for two red dots to momentarily flash back at you. Many times this will cause the animal to move, and you may be able to see her entire body more clearly.

If you do in fact see your pet, do not rush forward but instead take a moment to evaluate the situation, deciding if your dog is going to bolt or whether the animals is unable to flee. Once you feel confident that your dog is not going to dash into the night, move slowly to gain control and ease him towards a safe and contained location.

Tiger Line Physical Search

This is a tactic employed by law enforcement when they are looking for evidence at crime scenes. You are also looking for evidence, but it is in relation to your missing pet.

The physical evidence we are looking for will generally be in the nature of a collar, a tag, hair, blood, or signs of struggle. The most likely pet owners to use this technique are those who feel their pet may have met with a situation that ultimately may have caused serious injury or death, making it impossible for the pet to return. It can be because a pet is believed to have been hit by a car, injured in a fight, or caught by a predator.

For our purposes the Tiger Line is done with at least three people spaced no more than ten feet apart. This is preferably done at knee level in a high-probability area in the direction you feel or know the pet has traveled. The goal is to move together while visually and/or physically inspecting a small, defined territory no more than five feet to each side and in front of you. You are looking for any physical evidence like hair, blood, bone, nails, or signs of a struggle, which will appear as scratches or tears in the ground. You may also notice a defined trail evidenced by grass lying down or bushes and small branches pushed to the side where a predator may be entering and exiting the area. You do not need to use magnifying glasses or other magnification equipment, as the evidence should be more visible if you are within eighteen inches of the ground.

You should also be aware of coyote or other predator scat (bowel elimination), which can be present and close by if a predator is in the area. The scat will be different than dog or cat scat, as it will have fur, seed, berries, and possibly twigs in it as opposed to commercial dog or cat food.

This technique may sound tedious and slow, but most pet owners, with help from friends and family, can cover quite a lot of ground in a short time. For many, it can be closure to find evidence of death - or instill a sense of urgency if it is thought the pet is injured and may still be alive. In the case of a dog hit by a car, blood spatter or drops can show the direction of travel and a trail that leads to the pet.

There are additional instructions and suggestions for this technique at http://www.howtofindalost-dog.org/more-about-investigative-field-techniques.html.

Hire a Professional to Assist with Your Search

As the search for their dog unfolds, many pet owners call in professionals to help with their search. Having a professional trained in the recovery of missing dogs at your location leading and guiding your search greatly increases the likelihood of recovering your dog. Should you decide to bring in professionals, it is imperative to hire a company or individual that is actually skilled and trained in this specialty.

The missing-pet industry is a growing profession, but as of this writing, there are very few qualified professionals doing this work. For this reason, most professionals may have waiting lists depending on the time of year. Those of us who do this work are here to help people; telling a frantic or grieving pet owner that we cannot assist because of other appointments is one of the more difficult aspects of this job. For this reason, it is prudent to call and talk with a professional as soon as possible.

Ask, ask, and ask before hiring!

If you are considering a private investigator, pet detective, MAR Technician, search-and-rescue handler, or anyone else offering their services in the missing-pet world, I advise you to ask these questions before agreeing to hire anyone.

How long have you been studying or working the missing-dog crisis?

Answer: Should be at least a year, and they should have completed a physical course of study. One nonprofit organization on the Internet does a basic lost-pet course, and that is acceptable as a start, but it does not take the place of hands-on training and one to one mentoring.

Have you ever worked in private investigations or law enforcement or trained in search and rescue with a dog team?

Answer: This is not a requirement, but some form of investigative background is helpful. Most states require a private investigator or detective license to pursue the search for a missing pet. Licensed professionals will have been fingerprinted, passed a background check and fulfilled the experience and examination requirements for the state in which they are licensed. Most states also require a bond, insurance or both.

How many missing-dog cases have you worked?

Answer: Should be at least twenty but can be less if the other answers are positive. Make sure they have worked missing dogs, not just missing cats. If your dog is roaming, make sure they have expertise and success with this scenario.

Can you give me the names and phone numbers or e-mail addresses of three pet owners you have worked for?

Answer: You are only calling to see how the pet owner felt about the case. Many times the pet will be found because of the directions given by the professional. Caution: If the K9 handler or professional starts talking about confidentiality or protecting his or her client's privacy, be suspicious. This work is not crime fighting. Clients who have found their pets due to the help of a professional are more than happy to sing their praises.

Hiring a professional with a tracking dog team

Below are additional questions to ask if the professional works with a tracking dog team.

Note: Many private investigators may sub contract with certified K9 Handlers even if they do not have a dog team.

How long have you or your K9 Handler been handling tracking dogs?

Answer: Should have been a K9 handler for at least two years. This experience must be verifiable in some way. Learning how to work tracking dogs in a search takes years of experience. This skill set cannot be learned from a book or online class.

How many dogs do you or your K9 handler have on your team, and what do they do?

Answer: A professional will have at least two dogs on his or her team and at least one dog needs to be scent specific. A scent-specific dog will follow the scent of your dog and only your dog. The handler should talk to you about a scent article for his or her K9s to use in the search. If your dog is roaming, the handler must have at least two scent-specific dogs on his or her team. This is not a luxury; it is a requirement for success.

You should ask if the dogs are certified such as through MASDN, the Missing Animal Scent Dog Network.

Can you give me the name of another professional who handles tracking dogs and does this type of work who will give you a professional reference?

Answer: You cannot be successful as a K9 handler without background, training, and mentoring. The professional or K9 handler has to know someone. Once the person gives you the name of his or her reference, I suggest you Google the reference for assurance that his or her reference has actually worked a dog team and found missing dogs. There are many "online pet detectives" whose experience is based on the Internet and not boots on the ground investigations. You are looking for a successful work history and lost dog recoveries actually made by the reference. You also want assurance that the professional reference knows your intended lost dog expert and has worked with him or her on a face-to-face basis, not just over the phone, on Facebook, or through e-mail.

What You Should Expect

Although the goal is to find and recover your pet, there are four different outcomes that can result when hiring a tracking-dog investigative team. We are not wizards, and we don't have magic wands. We perform an investigation and search similar to that performed by law enforcement in missing-person cases.

The following are possible outcomes of a search and investigation:

- The investigation and search may result in the finding and recovery of your pet.
- The investigation and search may result in a direction of travel, the *most likely* escape scenario, and the pet's *most likely* experience. This is most likely in the roaming-dog scenario as well as a dog that has been recovered by a citizen and driven away in a car.
- The search and investigation may find that your pet has *most likely* met with an accident or some other tragedy that *most likely* caused his or her death.
- The K9 handler or investigator may be unable to detect what has happened to your pet due to a variety of reasons, which include, (but are not limited to), lack of a verifiable scent for your pet in the area, poor or contaminated scent article, possible sightings that are unverifiable based on the time allowed, or myriad other situations that are outside their control. *This outcome is highly unlikely if you have hired a real professional.*

Once you have decided to bring in professionals with tracking dogs, there are things that need to be prepared before the arrival of the team.

You Should Know a Little about Scent

There are many factors that affect scent and a tracking dog's ability to easily find and follow your pet's scent trail. Time, weather, heat, strong winds, heavy rains, ice, snow, nicotine from cigarette smoke, or heavy contamination by chemical, auto fumes, diesel, or gasoline can all contribute to a poor or difficult scent trail.

Contrary to popular belief, rain and moisture do not wash scent away but, in my experience, actually refresh the scent particles and make it easier for most scent dogs to detect and follow.

It is also important to note that pets, especially dogs, can travel great distances depending on how long they have been missing. The best tracking dogs are trained to follow the most recent scent trail they can find, but if your pet has been out in the escape area for a length of time, this can make detecting the correct track difficult and time-consuming for a K9 team. Be sure to alert the investigator or K9 handler if, prior to his disappearance, your pet spent time in the escape area so that adjustments can be made. For pets that have gone missing from their home or areas where the pets have spent time, it is crucial that the scent-specific dogs working on your case can differentiate older and newer scent trails. It does not matter if the tracking dog can follow the walking path your dog took two weeks before he went missing. The K9 must be able to find the last scent trail your dog took that resulted in his missing event.

The Scent Article

It is necessary to have an article that your missing pet has touched, lain on, used, played with, or somehow gotten scent on. The article must be free of scent from other animals. This article is how the scent dogs will sort out, from all the millions of scent particles in the atmosphere, those that belong to just your missing pet.

In our work, we do not use the actual scent article but instead have the pet owner prepare a group of scent pads that we present to the dog team. We use gauze for the scent pads, as this is the easiest material for most pet owners to obtain. Rolls of gauze cut into eight-inch lengths or gauze three by three or four by four in the package are also fine. Just make sure none of the material is scented with perfume, medication, or aroma.

Take at least six gauze pieces (if you are using packaged gauze pieces, take them out of the wrappers and unfold them), and roll them inside the selected scent article with your pet's scent. Place the article and the gauze inside a paper or plastic bag and seal the bag. The scent from the article will permeate into the gauze, and the K9 handler will open the bag and place the now-scented gauze in a plastic bag for presentation to the dogs at the beginning of the search. I prefer that the gauze and article be sealed together in the bag for at least four hours whenever possible.

Other items and preparations to have ready for the arrival of the tracking team are as follows:

- Signs and hanging materials: Have at least ten signs premade and ready to hang. As the search and investigation unfolds, it may be necessary to get public help when your pet's direction of travel and general location are discovered.

- Flyers: Have at least fifty, preferably colored but at least black and white, to hand to people as calling cards as the search proceeds.

- Color photo of your pet: If possible, place this photo in plastic or have it laminated. We will use this photo extensively as we continue to find members of the public who can confirm when your pet was in the area based on the trail, leads, and evidence discovered.

- Dress in comfortable clothing and running shoes if you are going to go with the K9 team. You may cover a lot of ground, especially with a roaming dog at large.

- Bring your missing pet's favorite smelly treat, a squeaky toy, a whistle, or anything that your pet may respond to that is sensory, auditory, or visual.

- Leashes, carrier, crate, collars, harness, and so on: Be prepared with a way to contain your pet should he be located during the search.

- If it is believed that the pet is at large and a location can be confirmed, be prepared to set up a feeding-and-comfort station as well as have humane traps available nearby.

- Call *all* local TV news stations and local newspapers. Make them aware that in the search for your missing pet, you have hired a specialized tracking-dog team. Create a story angle using facts and anything interesting or heartwarming about your pet or your situation. If you are working with a well-known or renowned investigator, so much the better. Expound and explain this to the news desk.

There are additional instructions and suggestions for hiring professional help at http://www.howto-findalostdog.org/more-about-investigative-field-techniques.html.

Attraction, Surveillance, and Capture Techniques

Encouraging Your Dog to Approach

If it is confirmed that your dog is in the area, the next step is to bring your dog to you.

Please remember that you cannot outsmart, outrun, or outdistance your dog; in most cases, the dog must make the decision to come to you. *Encourage your dog to approach, and give her time to make that decision.*

Go to the area where your dog has been sighted.

Find a place that is out of the traffic and public or well-used walking patterns. This is usually at the edge of a field, woods, park, creek, drainage, or open-space area.

Be prepared to be there for at least two hours. Some dogs have waited at the end of the woods for twelve hours before deciding to come out. The dog is traveling down a feral tunnel; she must make the transition back to domesticity, and that takes time.

What to bring:

- Bring a book, music, or anything to occupy your time. I recommend that after you have initially called for your dog, you read out loud, as this is an easy way to keep your voice light and your demeanor gentle. We want the sweet sound of your voice to travel out into the atmosphere. Sound and scent travel better in the early-morning hours, toward sunset, and at night, and these are the most likely times you will encounter your roaming dog if she is in the area.
- A chair or something to sit on is ideal.
- If your dog likes to ride in vehicles, bring the car or truck she is familiar with and leave the doors wide open.
- Treats, preferably your dog's favorites and/or something that is smelly and delicious. Canned cat food, tuna fish, Kentucky Fried Chicken, hot rotisserie chicken from the supermarket and hot hamburger meat still steaming are examples.
- Two leashes, one with slip lead and one with collar or harness, to contain your dog when she arrives and is under your control.

- If there is another pet in your household that your dog likes, bring that animal as a lure or magnet to attract your dog. Putting the lure dog or other animal on a long line or leash is best.
- If your dog is crate trained *and* enjoys her crate, set the crate out with its pillow or bedding.
- Bring any other items from your environment that the dog may recognize. Candles, music, guitar playing, and even cigarettes from a pet owner who smoked have all been successful in creating a pleasant and enticing memory that encouraged a frightened and shy dog to approach.

After deciding on a quiet spot near the area where your dog has been sighted, you need to set up the area to attract your dog.

- Set out your chair.
- Bring your book or the activity you will engage in while waiting.
- Set out your smelly treats and any other items that might encourage a scent or auditory memory for your dog.
- Set out your dog's crate if the dog is crate trained *and* likes her crate.
- Have the leashes or other containment ready and at hand.
- Have your vehicle parked nearby with the doors open if your dog likes to ride in that vehicle.

Our goal is to give the dog the opportunity to realize you are in the area. You must give the dog enough time to decide that all is well and she can approach.

If you try the above technique three different times for at least three hours, and you feel 80 percent sure your dog is nearby but is not approaching, you most likely will need to capture her with a humane trap or enclosure trap.

The following section explains the best ways to attract, capture, and recover a dog in this way.

Using a Magnet or Lure Animal

This is a very effective technique if the missing pet has a special animal friend or sibling that he or she likes. My experience is that a pet roaming at large or frightened and hiding is more likely to respond to an animal it knows than it is to respond to its actual owner.

We have successfully used female dogs in heat when dealing with a skittish Lothario; used the adult sibling of a frightened golden retriever at large on one hundred acres; and walked a cat on a leash down a path to lure her shy poodle friend out of the woods.

When a dog is at large, we frequently bring in a lure animal in hopes of attracting the lost dog close enough to begin to feed and coax it in as shown above. We prefer to use another dog that the missing pet knows, but we have used a cat to lure in a shy poodle. As mentioned, we have also used a female dog in heat, and while this can work it can also be very difficult to manage other male dogs who might be attracted. When given the option, we usually prefer to use an animal that is a friend and known to the missing dog.

The suggested technique is to walk the magnet animal around the area where we believe the missing dog is frequenting. I do not feel it is safe to tie a dog out in hopes of attracting the missing pet. In certain situations, pet owners have placed another pet from their household in a crate to attract their dog, but one must be very careful and diligent in watching over the situation from a distance.

This technique can be effective if the missing pet is in the area and is comfortable, fond, or excited about the lure animal.

There are additional instructions and suggestions for this technique at http://www.howtofindalost-dog.org/more-about-attraction.html.

Associative-Response Conditioning

This technique can be used to condition an animal that is wandering in an area to come to a comfort/feeding station or the dog's owner or guardian.

In my home, all animals are taught to respond to associative training techniques in relation to the "come" command. We do this as a precautionary measure in case the dog should ever become lost, injured, or separated from us while on the road.

Associative training is the imprinting of a sound or action through conditioning. In an emergency, the positive action desired is more likely to be achieved if some sort of association with the required action is imprinted with a sound or positive enforcer.

As stated, we achieve this training at home before our dogs are ever subjected to a missing situation. Below are the techniques we use to "quick condition" a pet that is fearful and at large.

Important: Do not use the "come" command or the pet's name for this conditioning. This is a separate sound from anything you have used for training up to this point in the pet's life.

The dinnertime song

The easiest time to imprint a technique is when you are getting ready to feed your pet. In our house we have the dinnertime song, which is simply the words "Dinner Time" repeated five times in a high voice while we prepare the dog's dinner. Sometimes we even dance and goof off, which excites the dogs and triggers memory more easily. In an emergency, should one of our dogs become separated from us, the dinnertime song is more likely to create a unique memory and thus the "call to action" than their basic obedience training. When an animal is panicked or injured or has been separated from the pack, it is more likely *not* to respond to basic training or commands. The positive feelings brought about by reinforcing and imprinting during feeding create a more long-lasting and effective response.

When a pet is at large, this same technique can be used combined with the process of getting tasty treats and food out of your car to take to a feeding station. I recommend that the process or sounds be continued as you set up the feeding station and at the humane trap if one is being used. It does not take dogs long to figure out that when the dinnertime song or other sound is used, they will be fed. This is the easiest way to imprint a desired response, which in our case is to *come* or at least come toward the area of the comfort-and-feeding station when the pet hears the song or sound. Many of our clients have spent hours, days, and weeks trying to get a frightened pet to respond to their pleas to come. Associative training encourages an automatic response based on basic instinct.

Other forms of imprinting and conditioning that can be used by pet owners in case of an emergency missing situation are:

Clucking the tongue: Like many equestrians use with horses. This is the technique I use when preparing a feeding-and-comfort station. I cluck three times about every three minutes or so throughout the whole process of preparing the meal and bringing in objects for the station.

Clicker training: A form of conditioned response that is generally associated with training in general. I prefer to have one action or sound just for a missing emergency. A clicker device or a cluck made by mouth is used to achieve the desired conditioned response.

Shaking a food or treat box: Many pet owners opt for this, as it is easy to do and many animals already associate this sound with treats and food. Shake a box of treats or use a shaker tool made with pebbles or rice in a plastic bottle for the associative "come to me" response.

Whistling: For years people have been calling their pets to dinner by whistling. It is tried and true, and the sound carries a long distance. Many shy and skittish animals will not respond and may run, so be careful with this. It is best to use this technique only if your pet is already *very* familiar with this form of response.

A positive command given in a high voice: Some people have an emergency-response word or command that they have reinforced with food or play reward. This is also effective but requires a separate training regime and is hard to teach when the dog is at large.

Clapping of hands: The sound carries over a great distance, and random or rhythmic clapping can be done as you place the food in the area. Again, be careful, as this is a loud noise and STARS dogs may flee from the noise.

Honking a horn: The sound a carries over a long distance, and each horn is fairly unique. This technique works in much the same way farmers call their cattle into feed as they arrive with the hay and grain. As you drive toward your feeding station, this can also be an effective alert or call to the dog.

Any sound that is associated with food or reward is great for this emergency measure. Regardless whether you see the roaming dog or not, it is most important to reinforce the words or sound repeatedly as you set about the tasks of setting out the food and fixing the comfort/feeding station.

Most of our clients, once they have experienced a missing situation, now use some word or technique to condition their pet for an emergency response in case they should ever need it again.

There are additional instructions and suggestions for this technique at http://www.howtofindalostdog.org/more-about-attraction.html.

Feeding-and-Comfort Stations

The most common scenario for this technique to be called into use is the roaming dog wandering at large or an animal living at large. The station itself is set up to bring the wandering pet to an area where it can expect food to be available.

There are numerous ways to use the station, but I prefer the technique that I have personally been the most successful with. It involves routine, associative training, and sumptuous smelly foods.

Location and placement of the station

The first task before deciding on the station and its placement is to have at least one confirmed sighting in the same area. Once a general location is decided upon, it is necessary to scope out the area and look for a place that is somewhat out of the way. Be aware of loose dogs, feral cats, and an overabundance of foot traffic. I prefer a place that is quiet and is in the path or traveling route of the roaming dog. A tree line, creek, easement, dirt road, and game trail used by wildlife can all be desirable placements.

Making it comfortable

I have personally had the most success with using a dog's bedding, toys, and the scent of other pets in the household. Many people prefer to use the scent of the pet owner, but I have had better results with the subject pet's items and the scent of other pets in the household. The pet is not responding to the owner at this point, so I have found that dogs at large are more likely to go to an animal friend than they are to their actual owner. I personally like to place the feces and urine, yes, the poo-poo, of other dogs in the household or dogs that the roaming dog knows, near the station. Dogs are very territorial, and they know who occupies their home territory. They are generally happy or at least curious to smell their comrades from home.

Making it yummy

I generally choose a smelly food like canned salmon, roasted chicken, or hot dogs mixed with dry kibble or rice. I prefer to place the concoction in the food bowl that the dog or other dogs in the household regularly use when at home.

Other suggested treats and food:

My favorite: hot dogs. They are smelly and last longer than most other foods.

But you can also use:

- Cheese
- Roasted or rotisserie chicken precooked from the grocery store
- Kentucky Fried Chicken
- Steaming-hot hamburger meat
- Arby's Roast Beef
- Rice mixed with any smelly, oily food
- Your dog's favorite treat
- Salmon
- Jack mackerel
- Sardines
- Tuna

Quantity

We are only trying to get the salivary juices working and encourage the dog to return. We are not trying to feed him or satisfy his hunger. Please remember, it is important for the dog to stay hungry so he can be captured. In most situations, it is extremely rare for a dog expire due to lack of food. We have had a six-pound Chihuahua on the roam in the snow for three weeks and a senior pointer who went for six weeks eating very little. They all survived and were captured with food as their motivator. So please think tempting morsels, not dining satisfaction.

When ready for use, the station should have:

1. Something with subject pet's scent on it like bedding or toys.
2. Sumptuous and tempting food.
3. A water bowl with water.
4. And the scent of another animal friend, whether the friend has walked around the station and marked the area or an item with the animal friend's scent is left at the station. Feces and urine from a doggie friend are great motivators. Also the litter box from the cats in residence if the dog lives in a home with cats.

Keeping out the Ants

One of the biggest dilemmas can be keeping the feeding station free from ants and other ground-crawling insects. We use a double-bowl system for this.

In general, ants do not swim.

You will need:

- A bowl that is larger than the food bowl
- The dog's food bowl
- Water

Pour at least two inches of water in the large bowl. Place the smaller food bowl inside the larger bowl with the water. Make sure the sides of the smaller bowl do not touch the larger bowl.

We have used this system many times and have kept the food ant free. We have had one ingenious species of ant that created a bridge with their bodies, but this has happened rarely. The average ant does not swim and cannot reach the food.

There are additional instructions and suggestions for this technique at http://www.howtofindalost-dog.org/more-about-attraction.html.

The Tuna Spritzer

This technique is used to spread food scent particles out into the ethers. Generally speaking, I prefer to use a fish-based substance soaked in water and then sprayed in the area where I want to attract a hungry roaming dog. Fish oils are very aromatic and tend to stay pungent longer than other food products.

1. Empty a can of tuna, mackerel, or salmon into a bowl of water, and let it sit for fifteen or twenty minutes.
2. Strain out the solid meats, and use them for your food bait.
3. Take the leftover water, and pour it into a spray bottle.

4. Spray the smelly water in a wagon-wheel pattern around the comfort station or trap. Spray up into the air, and let the droplets fall and carry on the air currents. Walk straight from the comfort station about thirty feet, spraying the smelly water into the air as you go.

5. You can also use this technique to lay a trail to an area you want the pet to come to.

Note: Many other critters will come too, so be prepared for uninvited guests.

Surveillance and Monitoring

If it is discovered that a cherished dog is roaming at large, this technique must generally be applied to establish if the dog is in fact in the territory, the times the animal is frequenting the area, and how often and long she stays.

This technique is best combined with a feeding station or humane trapping techniques to lure the animal for capture. The feeding station is described in the previous section.

There are two types of surveillance: surveillance done by a human or *manned surveillance* and automatic surveillance done by machines and cameras, *unmanned*. Most pet owners will do a combination ut today most surveillance of this type is done with motion-

an area is best done with a motion-sensor camera. Years
ars, but today most "big box stores" carry them for $49.95
sensitive cameras that send you a text photo every time
as" can also be found in the sporting-goods stores and
e-day delivery on these, and they are very competitive

Stealth Cam   096 F   08-28-2012 14:04:58

When placing the camera, it is best to fasten the camera to a solid box, stand, or tree. The camera must be very solidly stationed. Electrical tie wraps and bungee cords can be used to attach the camera and stabilize it, and there are also commercial locking systems that attach the camera while locking it in place for security.

It is best to position the camera according to the directions for distance. The camera will take a picture whenever something comes into its sensor range. Depending on brand and technology, these cameras are fairly accurate, but you may find that you get many pictures of many different animals. That's OK and is to be expected. If you go three days in one location and there are no sightings of the dog/your pet does not appear in the photos, it's possible that you need to rethink the strategy for this location.

Once you see your dog in the photo or you know he is coming to the station to eat, it is time to bring out the humane trap and add it to the station. See the next section.

Manned surveillance: Bring a book but be prepared to look up frequently. Stay alert and awake. Most people who opt for this technique use it during the day when it is easier to see. Your scent will carry to the pet, so it is important to stay downwind and at least one hundred feet away. It is best that your dog not think he is being observed, even if it is by you. At this point you may have already discovered that your pet is not responding to your calls and presence, so initially it is best to allow the pet the freedom to approach the food on its own with no intervention from you. Patience is key here.

I recommend you sit in an area downwind of the feeding station and that you use some type of magnification like binoculars or a telephoto lens on a camera.

Take note of what you see

Whether on camera or on site, take note of your dog's condition and behaviors while on camera or in view.

- Does he appear thin or the same?
- Do you see any noticeable any injuries?
- Is the fur matted or does it have a lot of debris in it?
- Does the pet appear muddy or wet?
- Does he still have on his collar or ID (if he left with ID on)?

You are trying to learn the pet's condition while noting characteristics that may explain where he is traveling.

Note the time he appears and how long he stays and if he pays attention to any other object you have brought to the station for his enjoyment.

- Does he lie down?
- Does he play with a toy?
- Does he appear to notice the scent, urine, or poo-poo left by pets he knows (that you have left at the station)?
- Does he stay very long?
- Does he leave and then come back?

You see your dog while on manned surveillance

The tough call is whether or not to make yourself known after your dog appears or starts eating. This is tough because he may bolt as soon as he hears a voice—even yours. If he does bolt, he may not return to eat at the station, thus eliminating the possibility of capturing him at this location later.

A good rule of thumb: If the dog has not bolted from you and he approaches and picks up a toy, or better yet, lies down on bedding or clothing, you may consider quietly calling him in your inside affectionate voice. Do not yell for him or in any way raise your voice. Calm and quiet. If he jumps up, bolts, or acts frightened, stop calling and hunker down quietly so he does not leave the area. He may return later.

Once you know your dog has come to the station to eat, it is time to introduce the humane trap and add it to the station.

There are additional instructions and suggestions for this technique at http://www.howtofindalost-dog.org/more-about-surveillance-and-monitoring.html.

The Humane Trap

When a pet is at large and is not allowing anyone to approach, many times it is necessary to utilize a self-closing wire cage trap, commonly referred to as a humane trap.

A humane trap made for a dog must be big enough for the dog to enter easily. A dog trap will be at least twenty-seven inches high and four feet long. The dog must be able to walk in the trap without his head, whiskers, or ears touching the top or sides.

Note: Many breeds or crosses may not respond to this type of trap and may need an enclosure trap. Dogs in the herding group and the sporting group may not enter these traps due to their intelligence and ability to reason. Also, any dog that can get food on their own may not be motivated enough to go in a trap.

There are several types of dog traps available. Most professionals use traps made by Tru-Catch due to their size and reliability; however, most pet owners use whatever is available from their local animal control or rescue group. Many shelters and animal-welfare groups rent out traps on a daily or weekly basis. Some feed stores also do this. It is generally best to check into the rental of these traps before you need them. Once you are in the process of surveillance and feeding stations, it is prudent to already have the trap in your possession ready to be placed. Nothing is worse than having a verification that your wandering pooch has shown up twice in the same place over the last two days, and when you call for the trap, you are told there is a waiting list. Be prepared, and if there is a list, be aware that some pet retailers and feed stores do sell them as do some Internet sites.

It is best to learn to set the trap at home before you need it at your location. Most come with directions, but some rentals may not have the instructions any longer. So perform your due diligence ahead of time. Test the door and trip mechanism before leaving to make sure they work properly. Nothing worse than a trap meant for a small dog that takes a polar bear's weight to trip it, or the reverse - a mechanism that will not hold the door open in a light breeze.

In my experience we *don't get second chances with traps*. If a dog has a bad experience with one and it doesn't close all the way or the door trips early and catches a paw or the tail of a fleeing pet, the chance that the pet will return and try again is almost nonexistent. So practice and be certain everything works.

Placing the trap

Strategic placement of the trap is crucial to your success. It is also important to the safety of any animal you inadvertently trap.

- Be aware of weather conditions and plan around it. Do not leave an animal in the heat or freezing cold. Figure the elements into your strategic placing of the trap.
- Noisy or nosy children, well-meaning adults who want to help too much, loose dogs, or a feral cat population nearby can create the need for you to change your location and strategy.
- If possible, it is best if the trap is in a place where people you know or have just gotten to know due to their proximity to your sighting location can see the trap without the necessity of stepping out of their house.
- If you are placing on private property, and we usually are, you must have the resident's permission. One of my best locations was next to a creek bed in an exclusive housing subdivision. Three new friends acquired during the search for the dog I was trying to trap had decks that were fifty to two hundred feet away from the trap. On the third day, our roaming dog arrived near the trap, and all the neighbors saw him. The next night we set the trap, and the dog arrived for dinner and walked right in. The pet owner was called, and Fido was out of the trap in less than fifteen minutes.

Note: In this success story, the trap was tied open until the dog had actually entered the trap to eat at least once. This is a tough call and one that takes a lot of patience. Many people prefer to keep the trap set from the very beginning in case the pet does not come back to eat. I usually prefer to let the pet get comfortable first because of my prior concerns about the pet having a bad experience with the trap and never being able to use the trap again for the animal. Decide wisely on your location and the placement of the trap.

Preparing the trap

Most animals do not like to walk on wire, which is what the floor of most traps is made of. I prefer a camouflage flooring over the wire of some type. My favorite is natural grasses, leaves, twigs, and dirt, but you have to be careful with this, as the stuff can get into your mechanism. A blanket or burlap bag will also work. I also recommend placing the trap on something instead of the bare ground. A bath mat or small throw rug is great, as the trap will not slip or move around as easily. I like to then cover the mat or rug with dirt, leaves, and so on and make it look as natural as possible.

Covering the trap itself is usually not desirable unless you use something that is natural and from the area. Pine boughs, branches, straw, and hay all work well in making the trap look more like an outdoor cave or borough in the brush. Do not use tarps or blankets to cover the trap as any noise made by the cover flapping in the breeze can frighten off an anxious roaming dog.

Sweet smell of home

I also prefer to have the pleasant scent of home in or near the trap. That can be the scent of the person the pet is most bonded to, a favorite toy, or my personal favorite, the scent of another pet in the household that the roaming animal enjoys. Having the favorite pet friend walk around the trap or placing it inside temporarily is ideal, as it will leave its scent. I have had pet owners use dirty cat litter, favorite food bowls, or anything that is not bulky or too large. The animal must be able to walk in easily, and the door to the trap must be able to close smoothly and easily.

Outdoor dining

All of the above are meant as comfort to the pet, but he is coming for food, and it is food we must provide. If you have been setting a smelly table such as the feeding station and that has attracted him to the area, use the same attractive food. When placing the food in the back of the trap, make sure the dog has to step all the way into the trap to reach the food. It is OK to dribble some of the tasty stuff in front of the trap and inside the door. Dribbles are not pieces of food. They are very small enticing morsels leading the way to the grand dinner inside.

Double-check the stability of the trap before you leave. Push down on the top and make sure it does not move. If the trap wiggles, go back to the drawing board. Most animals will not enter something that feels unstable.

Think safety for all concerned

Someone must check the trap regularly at least every four hours throughout the night and day, and this is in great weather. Other animals interested in your dining setup may also enter the cage and become trapped. For visual ease, I recommend adding a reflective or glow-in-the-dark tape to the front of the trap door. When the trap is closed, the reflective or glow-in-the-dark item will show clearly from a distance. The tape is *not*, however, a replacement for walking up to the trap every four hours. Do not ever leave the trap longer than this. If you must be gone and the trap is not going to be monitored, remove the food, close the trap door and begin again when someone responsible can monitor the trap. Whoever is going to check the trap must know how to release it for those animals accidentally caught in your efforts.

Note: When the weather is less than perfect, it is best to never leave the trap unattended for longer than two hours. Great care must be taken to ensure that an animal does not become hurt or overexposed to the weather and climate.

When your beloved pet is inside the trap

Do not run up to the trap and throw open the door. Approach your dog slowly and with caution. He will most likely appear different at first and may need some space. Nothing is worse than a gleeful pet owner who finds that Cujo has taken over her docile pup while he was on the lam. Talk to the animal and if possible sit for a while with him before moving the trap. Even if he is overjoyed to see you, *do not open* the trap.

It is best to take the entire trap with the dog inside to an area that is enclosed before you take her out. After all your work, you do not want the pet to escape your grasp and hit the road again. Take your time and allow the dog to acclimate to the surroundings, and then open the trap door in an enclosed area where the dog cannot escape.

Bushnell Ⓜ my LPP cam 75F23C ◑ 10-21-2015 18:06:51

Also, it is best if only the people who are emotionally bonded to the dog are allowed to be in the area while the dog is being released from the trap. It is best for young children to stay away from the dog for a few hours until it is clear that the dog is beginning to recover from his ordeal. The roaming dog has been in a constant state of high alert during the missing event and journey; waiting to celebrate the dog's return to the family should wait until it is clear the dog is acclimating and responsive to his domestic training and usual patterns.

There is more information about steps and precautions in your dog's return in Section 4 of this book titled "Home Sweet Home: What to Do after Your Pet Is Home."

There are additional instructions and suggestions for this technique at http://www.howtofindalost-dog.org/more-about-capture.html.

The Enclosure Trap

W_hen a dog is too big or will not enter a humane trap, we use this alternative._ This technique will generally require a manned or active capture.

There are breeds and individual dogs that do not respond to humane traps. My experience is that the more intellectual the dog, the less likely it is that he or she will enter a humane trap. Shetland Sheepdogs, German Shepherds, Border Collies, Boxers, Australian Shepherds, Dachshunds, and any dog crossed with one of these breeds are the dogs least likely to enter a humane trap. With these dogs and many others, we use an enclosure trap.

What is an enclosure trap?

It is basically what it says it is. It is an area that encloses the dog and allows you to shut a gate or door and capture him after he has entered. We have used backyards, a car port surrounded by chicken wire, garages, a chicken coop, gardens, and the most popular, the portable chain-link kennel you can buy at a number of large feed store retailers.

All these enclosed options are larger areas that a dog is more likely to enter. Of all the enclosed processes we encounter, capturing a dog in a nearby fenced yard or area is the easiest. Unfortunately, in most roaming-dog situations this is not always feasible or available.

You must use the same attraction techniques detailed earlier, but in this case, you must place the food as far away from the gate or door as possible. This is usually done with an active or manned capture to trigger the gate. There are now some trigger mechanisms available on the Internet, which can be shipped overnight in some cases. See the "Resources" section of the companion website for possible suppliers.

There are additional instructions and suggestions for this technique at http://www.howtofindalostdog. org/more-about-capture.html.

Home Sweet Home...
Aftercare Suggestions

Congratulations, you did it, and we always knew you could.

There are some things you need to consider now that your dog is home; some may surprise you, and some may not.

Many pet owners feel it best to get their dog to their Veterinarian as soon as they recover or find the dog. I personally have mixed feelings on this. If the dog appears to be in distress or is severely dehydrated, then of course, head to the Vet.

When a pet owner calls to say, "I have her!" I generally recommend taking the dog home for at least twenty-four hours. A roaming dog needs time to readjust to domesticity, and I do not believe that prodding, needles, or tests help that reentry process.

It is better for the dog to come home to a quiet homecoming. On too many occasions, concerned pet owners have taken their dog to an overzealous Vet who felt it necessary to run every test under the sun and then keep the dog at the clinic. This is not in the best interest of the dog unless the dog is ill, injured or in distress.

Tips and Suggestions

Remember, a dog that has been roaming is likely to do it again when frightened or the instinct to flee wells up again. So it is best to keep Fido away from the doors and windows for a while.

Do not expect your dog to act overjoyed to see you. She will return to her normal routine but it may take anywhere from several hours to several days. Most dogs are aloof and indifferent for a while before they come to some place in the process where they recognize you and their old way of life. Do not be disappointed if the dog that used to jump up and give you sloppy kisses is now not even interested in sitting in your lap or coming near.

Give your dog space and time. She will resume life soon, but for now allow the dog space. She has been on her own; noise and activity are not what she needs, so hold off the well-wishers and welcome-home parties until the dog is responding to you with affection and without fear or indifference.

Feeding

How long the dog has been gone should be the deciding factor in how much food and water to give to the dog. Call your Vet and ask for his or her advice about this. I recommend one tablespoon of food for each ten pounds of body weight two to three times a day. Boiled chicken with rice seems to be fine for most dogs. Go with what your Vet suggests. Water may be rationed in the first six hours, but I have never known a dog to get sick from too much water after returning from most roaming situations.

Behaviors

Your dog has lived as if wild for some time, so do not be surprised if your house-trained dog now has accidents or lifts his leg in the house when he did not do it before. The training will come back with gentle reminders.

Many dogs come back with a new interest in food, and some can have food aggression and frantic bolting and gulping of their food. Usually this behavior goes away, though some pet owners have remarked that this behavior stays longer than other feral-like actions.

Most dogs are a little standoffish at first with other pets in the household. On some occasions, I have known a returning dog to attack what used to be a much-loved playmate upon return. Prudence suggests keeping the dog separated from the other pets in the household for the first day or so, especially if there are any signs of growling or aggression.

The Big Question: Could My Dog Do This Again?
Answer: Yes.

It is best if you treat your dog like an escape artist for the first six months to a year after his recovery. It was instinct and survival that kept him out, and that does not go away once awakened. In one case, a small Shih Tzu would race toward his car whenever he was frightened after his recovery, but I have known others that would bolt for the door as if safety was out in the bush instead of the backyard.

The dog should not be allowed off leash in public for a good long time. When I see the experience most people go through to get their dogs back, I am surprised if they ever let the dog off leash again.

Enjoy your dog and the return to your old life—sort of. The dog that came home is not the same dog that left. Most of us are surprised at how our dogs survive when out in the great big world, and we gain a new respect for the canine that shares our bed and life.

Enjoy this new relationship with your amazing dog.

Congratulations to you both.

Prevention

Over four million pets a year go missing. There are many reasons, situations, and circumstances surrounding these missing events. In some cases, a dog goes missing due to a tragic accident or mishap. Other times a gregarious dog escapes while other situations may be related to a reactive STARS dog. Regardless the circumstance, there are measures that can be taken that can prevent the crisis or at least will hasten the recovery of the missing dog.

Below are the most common situations we encounter that result in a dog going missing. I have suggested techniques, equipment, and actions for the prevention of these specific situations.

The Most Common Ways in Which Dogs Go Missing
Eighty percent of our cases are dogs that go missing from a place they are unfamiliar with and is outside their home territory.

Dogs Lost during Transport in a Vehicle
Whether lost during a family vacation, a rescue transport to a new home, or escape from an auto accident, dogs lost during transport in a vehicle is a common occurrence. The highest percentage of dogs that are lost from a vehicle are loose and unrestrained.

Suggestions for Prevention
Crating the dog: Many of the cases we work involve dogs lost while being transported in a vehicle. In some cases, the dog escapes due to an auto accident while in others the dog maneuvers its way out a door or window. Regardless the circumstance, crating the dog in a crate during transport will alleviate many of the most common transport escapes.

Inside restraints: Second to crating a dog is the seat-belt harness restraint. Although this measure is second in desirability, it is better than allowing the dog to be loose inside a vehicle.

Leave the leash on the dog: As you go to get your dog from the vehicle, pay attention to the dog's behavior and firmly grip the leash before opening the door to get the dog out of the vehicle.

Bringing the dog into a place the dog fears: Many dogs flee in the parking lot of a veterinary hospital, dog-grooming salon, or boarding facility. Regardless the reason, many reactive and shy dogs are petrified of these situations and will struggle mightily to escape. At any given moment, we always have at least one case we are working where the dog escaped either going into or leaving one of these locations. Crating the dog while in the vehicle, leaving the leash on and not opening the door until you have the leash firmly in hand can alleviate most of these situations. If you have a small dog, carry the crate inside the building with the dog inside as a further precaution.

Dog Escapes from a Boarding Facility or While in the Care of Someone Other Than the Pet Owner
Many dogs lose confidence and become highly reactive when brought to a boarding facility or when left in the care of someone who is not their primary caretaker or guardian. These dogs can become

frightened, and as their fears escalate and their adrenaline rises, they frantically try to escape and many times are successful.

Suggestions for Prevention

Look at the facility for escape possibilities. When at all possible, it is important to look at the boarding and care arrangement for safety.

- A safe boarding facility will have a multiple gate or door system, so a fleeing dog has to pass through many doors before it reaches the street or vast beyond.
- When the dog is taken out for play or potty, it is desirable that yard be enclosed with a six-foot no-climb fence. Facilities that take dogs out to potty on a leash in an open public area with no fencing are the least desirable as more dogs escape from these situations than any other boarding mishap.
- When dogs are moved from place to place inside the facility, check to see that they are double leashed to avoid accidents or the dog slipping the lead from its neck.
- Many boarding operations remove the dog's collar when they come into boarding to prevent the collar from becoming caught in the fence. The difficulty arises when a dog does escape and is now in the big world without identification. Facilities that remove the collar should provide a paper collar with a phone number just in case.

Tell the facility or the caregiver about your dog and what you expect:

- The staff or caretakers should be given instructions on your dog's behavior and fears.
- Reactive and less confident dogs not comfortable in the care of strangers should never be left alone in a yard or contained area while the dog is being cared for. This includes dogs that are left with family members they know.
- In an emergency, tell the staff or caregiver that should your dog escape and is not captured immediately, you are to be called within ten minutes of the dog's missing event. Explain that the staff should not chase your dog; instead give them suggestion on how to get your dog to come to them. These instructions should all be in writing.

Dog Escapes While Being Walked on or off Leash

When a dog goes missing near its home, most of the time it is while being walked. Sometimes an accident occurs, but most of the time, the dog is startled by something and bolts.

Suggestions for Prevention

Ability and cognizance: Not only should the martingale collar be used with a six-foot leash, but the individual walking the dog should also have the ability and cognizance to know what to do in an emergency. Many dogs escape while children are walking them and something unforeseen occurs such as loose dogs approaching causing the dog on the leash to become frightened. It is a good rule of thumb that children under ten only be allowed to walk a dog with an adult present and within very close proximity.

Where to walk: It is always better to know the area where you walk your dog as opposed to setting out into areas where you do not know what you will encounter. This is particularly important with reactive dogs who bolt when frightened.

Hiking and off leash: Many of our cases are dogs that go missing when they are off leash. In almost all situations, the pet owner will tell us that their dog has always been fine in the past being off leash but on this day the dog reacted different. Dogs that escape while hiking in wilderness areas are by far some of the toughest cases to solve.

- If you are a hiker and your dog is your hiking partner, consider the risks before beginning each hike.
- It is imperative that you are 100 percent confident of your dog's recall.
- If your dog has any tendency toward STARS behavior, is prone to bolting when frightened, or is under fourteen months old, I highly recommend you do not walk the dog off leash in any situation, especially in wilderness areas.

Dog Goes Missing from Home of Pet Owner, Rescuer, or New Adopter

Suggestions for Prevention

The backyard: By far the most effective enclosure to keep a dog safe is a six-foot or higher privacy fence with a locked gate. This fencing allows a dog to be unseen by the public as well as a secure enclosure that he cannot escape. Of course the fence must be maintained with no missing boards, and the area at the bottom should discourage digging for those escape artists who might try to dig out.

The stolen dog: Privacy fencing is one of the best deterrents for theft. This type of fencing does not allow a dog to be seen by random opportunists who might want to take a dog they find desirable for cause or breed.

Dog Escapes from a Dog Park

Suggestions to Consider

Does your dog enjoy this activity? There is strong encouragement for all city dwellers to frequent the dog park. It is important to recognize why you are bringing your dog to a dog park and on the top of that list should be because the dog enjoys it. Some of my dogs enjoy the dog park while others find it very threatening and/or overstimulating. Taking a reactive or less confident dog to a dog park to socialize or get him *used to it* when the dog is clearly in distress is a mistake. Not all dogs enjoy the dog park, and not all dogs should go to a dog park.

Each visit to the dog park should be evaluated before your dog is turned loose inside the fenced enclosure. Look around to decide if the current atmosphere inside the dog park is inviting, safe, and acceptable to you and your dog.

- Are there any dogs that appear to be out of control or overly zealous?
- Are there humans inside who are oblivious to the trouble their dog is causing?
- Is there a pack mentality going on where one or two dogs are being chased by a group of dogs?
- Is there a shy dog trying to get away from the activity inside?
- Is there anyone posing a threat inside the enclosure, including children who do not appear to have appropriate boundaries or parental guidance?
  The action and activity inside the dog park on any given day is crucial to preventing an escape event.

Plan Ahead - Basic Equipment & Techniques

Many times, when working a case, we have found that the missing dog crisis could have been averted by using the following basic equipment and trained attraction technique.

Collars: The safest and most effective collar to use when walking or moving a dog from place to place is the martingale collar. The collar can be made from a variety of materials. This collar is the least likely of all collars for a dog to slip out of. This collar is highly recommended for all dogs that are reactive, exuberant, or dogs that exhibit STARS behaviors.

Leashes: A six-foot leash is easier for most people to use than a four foot. A six-foot leash allows the dog some freedom and is less likely to create a situation where the dog is struggling to keep from being dragged or overly restrained due to the length of the leash. The most common leash to create a disaster is the retractable leash. More dogs go missing due to the malfunction or an emergency created by this form of leash. I do not recommend the use of a retractable leash at any time or for any reason.

The Dinnertime Song:

Enforcing your recall: As explained earlier in the book, in the "Associative Conditioning Response" section, we condition our dogs to the dinnertime song. This conditioned recall is very simple and involves the words "Dinner Time" repeated five times in a high voice while we prepare the dog's dinner. Sometimes we even dance and goof off, which excites the dogs and triggers a memory response more easily. In an emergency, should one of our dogs become separated from us, the dinnertime song is more likely to create a unique memory and thus the "call to action" than their basic obedience training. When an animal is panicked or injured or has been separated from the pack, it is more likely *not* to respond to basic training or commands. The positive feelings brought about by reinforcing and imprinting during feeding creates a more long-lasting and effective response.

There are additional instructions and suggestions for this technique at http://www.howtofindalostdog. org/more-about-prevention.html.

References & Resources

Glossary

Note: This is a book about missing dogs. All of the terms below are described as they relate to that subject. Some terms and words may have different or other meanings outside the missing dog context.

Accidental Displacement: One of the Nine Scenarios wherein a dog is accidentally displaced to a location besides its home, usually by transport in a vehicle or moving object. Dogs that may wander into an open vehicle or boxcar on a train are examples of this scenario. This is an uncommon scenario. Also known as Accidental Transport.

Accidental Transport: One of the Nine Scenarios wherein a dog is accidentally displaced to a location besides its home usually by transport in a vehicle or moving object. Dogs that may wander into an open vehicle or boxcar on a train are examples of this scenario. This is an uncommon scenario. Also known as **Accidental Displacement**.

Aerial Diagnostic or Aerial Review or Aerial Analysis: One of the techniques used to perform a case review and develop a recovery strategy.

Air Scenting: This technique is used by all dogs but some dogs more than others. In our work, we refer to air scenting when the dog is working a scent cone, running to the scent trail, or running to the subject. They are not following the subject's trail but pick up the scent from the atmosphere.

Alert: A trained or natural behavior a dog will give in certain situations. We use many types of alerts. There are negative alerts, find alerts, driveway alerts, decomposition alerts, coyote alerts and other alerts the scent dogs need to communicate with their handler.

Associative Words: A technique we employ when talking with pet owners to help them bring forth or remember a scent article with their pet's scent that they cannot remember.

C4T: This simple acronym describes behaviors a dog may exhibit. These canines can be confident, calm, courageous, cooperative, and most of all trusting of humans. When a C4T dog goes missing, it is more likely to allow approach by a human than a STARS dog (shy, timid, aloof, reserved, or skittish).

Case: The term investigators use to describe the process and analysis of finding a missing dog. The work in its entirety.

Case Review: A review of a missing pet's case that includes Profiling, Aerial Diagnostic, Missing Event, Geography/Environment Analysis, Population Density, and Population Centers. All these factors help to develop a recovery strategy.

Confirmed Sighting: A sighting of a dog seen by a witness is the subject missing dog. The sighting can be confirmed visually due to unique identifiers, by a photo of the dog taken by witness, or scent-specific tracking dogs may have alerted to the subject's dog scent as being present at the sighting.

Contamination: The term we use when a scent article has more than one animal's scent on it.

Crittering: A broad-based term usually meaning the tracking dog is distracted by game, wildlife, or an environmental factor. Reading the dog correctly and consistently will help the handlers know and correct when their dog is crittering.

Decomp or Decomposition: Refers to any and all remains of a deceased animal.

Delusional K9 Handler: A phrase used to describe an inexperienced handler who believes his or her scent dog is presenting information that is incorrect or not there. This can generally be attributed to the handler's error in reading his or her tracking-dog team and being overzealous due to inexperience.

Direction of Travel—DOT: The direction that a subject has traveled.

Drive Away: Term used when a missing pet is recovered by a citizen and driven away in a car or other vehicle.

Environmental Analysis: Same as **Geography Analysis**. An analysis of the terrain and environment where the pet is missing.

Escape Event: The incident that occurred leading to a dog going missing. Same as **Missing Event**.

False Trail: See **Phantom Trail**.

Feline Profiling: Similar to K9 Profiling but for cats. Technique to arrive at summary strategy conclusion based on cats' behavior and history.

Feral Dog: A dog that was born or is living on its own. For our purposes, this dog does not appear to have an owner.

Feral Behavior: Behavior that resembles the actions and activities of a feral dog or its feral cousins, the wolf and coyote.

Finders Keepers: One of the five situations that can occur when a dog is found by a citizen or member of the public. The finder of this dog elects to keep the dog.

Found by Citizen: One of the Nine Scenarios describing a situation where a dog is found and recovered by a citizen. Also referred to as **Recovered by Citizen**.

Game Camera: A motion sensitive camera placed strategically to photograph passing wildlife or other subjects like a roaming dog.

Geographic Analysis: An analysis of the terrain and environment where the pet is missing. Also called **Environmental Analysis**.

Google Earth: An online program used for environmental and terrain analysis.

Guardian: An individual or group who are responsible for the actions and care of a dog. It could be a pet owner, a rescue, a foster parent, transporter, or other entity who is responsible for the care, custody, and control of a dog. The position can be fluid such as with a dog in a rescue organization.

Held for Reward: One of the five situations that can occur when a dog is found by a citizen or member of the public. The finder retains the dog to collect the reward. Also called **Recovered for Reward**.

Highest Search Probability Theory: The most probable situation based on experience and case histories.

High Value Treat or Food: A desirable food item that is attractive to all dogs. Meat, Salmon and other carnivore-type food stuffs are usually considered high value but this can also describe a specific treat that a particular dog likes.

Home by Phone: A K9 Profiling and Aerial Diagnostic System designed by Karin TarQwyn and available to pet owners with a missing dog through Karin TarQwyn or Lost Pet Professionals. The name and system are copyrighted and trademarked by Karin TarQwyn.

Intentional Displacement: One of the Nine Scenarios wherein a dog is intentionally displaced to a location besides its home. Dogs captured by animal control are the classic example of this scenario, but other incidences could involve neighbors, family members, or people who may or may not know the dog or its owner. Differs from the stolen dog as this dog is off its property when displaced.

K9 Profiling: Terminology that describes the process used to analyze a missing dog's behavior.

Missing Animal Response Technician—MAR Technician: The title and acronym used by individuals who have taken and passed a lost pet class. Most MAR Technicians achieve their certification through an online class, but some have been certified by other means.

Missing Dog Crisis: A phrase used to describe when a much-loved dog is missing.

Missing Event: The incident that occurred when the dog went missing. Also called the **Escape Event.**

Negative Scent: The subject pet has not been in the area and there is no scent.

Negative Sighting: A sighting comes in of a dog that looks similar to the subject missing dog, but factors determine it is not a confirmed or positive sighting. It is not the missing dog we are looking for.

Nonspecific Scent dog: This dog finds a specific species or item like all raccoons, all humans, all mushrooms, and so forth. It does not differentiate between individuals of the same species. We do not use dogs like this in our work.

Pet Detective: Made popular by the movies of the same name, this term is now a catch all phrase for anyone involved in the search for missing pets. Many individuals using this phrase are not and have never been licensed investigators or detectives. The term is used freely within the missing-pet industry and by the media.

Phantom Trails: A trail a tracking dog chooses to work, but it is not the trail of the subject he is being asked to work. We never want Phantom Trails, and we do everything to prevent this. Also called a **False Trail.**

Point Last Seen—PLS: The last place or point where a dog was seen.

Point of escape (POE): The point from where the missing dog escaped.

Population Centers: A review of areas where the pet is missing where the population is higher. In a rural area, it is where the citizens in the area travel to for shopping and to fulfill other needs of life.

Population Density: A review of the population in the area where the pet is missing.

Positive Scent: The subject pet has been at the location and the tracking dog has scent.

Predator: In the missing-dog world, this describes any animal that may choose pets as prey. Animals and birds in this category are coyotes, foxes, mountains lions, bobcats, fisher cats, wolves, owls, hawks, falcons, and eagles. The most common predator in the United States that may choose pets as prey is the coyote.

Primary Scent Article: After reviewing all the scent articles a pet owner has, this is the article the K9 handler feels most confident in. This is the article presented to the scent dogs.

Proofing: A term used to describe the technique used to check that a tracking dog is on a scent trail. Usually the dog is given a negative scent article to make sure he is on scent before continuing on with that trail.

Proofing the Primary Scent Article: A technique used to confirm that the scent article selected is effective and uncontaminated.

Puppy Runaway: The term used to describe the beginning trails a new tracking dog will be given to learn how to track or follow a scent trail. Can also be used to motivate a tracking dog working a long trail.

Quick Conditioning: Terminology use to describe a fast training technique to be used in an emergency such as in the attraction of a STARS dog on the roam.

Reading the Dog: The primary and most important part of working with a tracking dog is being able to understand what he is doing at any given moment. Many handlers are not skilled at this, and they end up with wandering tracking dogs taking them on walks and **Phantom Trails**.

Recovery Strategy: The summary we reach after a case review or an on location search with a K9 Team.

Recovered by Citizen: One of the Nine Scenarios describing a situation where a dog is found and recovered by a citizen. Also referred to as **Found by Citizen.**

Recovered for Reward: One of the five situations that can occur when a dog is found by a citizen or member of the public. The finder retains the dog to collect the reward. Also called **Held for Reward**.

Rescuer Rehome: One of the five situations that can occur when a dog is found by a citizen or member of the public. The finder elects to find a home for the dog.

Reward: A monetary or valuable asset or service given to a finder or witness for returning a missing dog or helping in the recovery efforts.

Roaming-Dog Scenario: One of the most common of the Nine Scenarios. This scenario describes a dog that is wandering or roaming on its own. This is generally a STARS dog that is loose and can be untrusting of humans.

Roaming Dog: Describes a dog that is wandering and is off its owner's or guardian's property.

Running to Scent: When a dog air scents his way to the actual trail the subject has traveled.

SAR: abbreviation for search and rescue. See **Search and Rescue**

Samaritan Recovery or Rescue: One of the five situations that can occur when a dog is found by a citizen or member of the public. The finder recovers the dog with the intent of finding the dog's owner.

Scenario Deduction: The summary arrived at during a case review or search that explains which of the Nine Scenarios a missing pet is most likely experiencing.

Scent Article: The item with the missing pet's scent that we will present to the tracking-dog team.

Scent Cone: Generally used in reference to the cone of scent that disperses from an object. The cone is narrower and "hotter" closest to the subject. Many scent dogs will spiral and cast as they work in to a subject

Scent Detection Dog or Scent Discrimination Dog: This is the term for all dogs that work to detect and decipher scent.

Scent Scan: We use this technique to find out if a sighting is negative or positive. In an advanced search, we use it to determine boundaries of a wandering dog.

Search Dog: The term used to describe SAR dogs. We do not use this term for our dogs as this term is used to explain dogs that look for people as opposed to pets. The search for a missing person is far different than the search for a lost pet, and it is important to clarify this to the public. Many times SAR dogs go out on a lost pet case and they have no results that is because a true search dog will be proofed against animal scent and only look for the human scent on the scent article. Scent dogs trained to find lost dogs, do just the opposite; they eliminate the human scent.

Search and Rescue: Search and rescue (SAR) is the search for and provision of aid to *people* who are in distress or imminent danger.

Search Protocol: The steps necessary to conduct a search for a missing pet.

Seized for Resale: One of the five situations that can occur when a dog is found by a citizen or member of the public. The finder of the dog recovers the dog with the intention being to sell the dog.

Sighting: A witness reports seeing a dog that matches or looks similar to our subject missing dog.

Sightings Journal Form or Sightings Query Form: A form with questions used to query potential witnesses who have reported seeing the missing dog or have information in regard to the dog's whereabouts. The form is saved creating a journal of information.

Scent Specific or Specific Scent dog: The scent dog will follow the specific scent of a given subject. A scent article or scent placement is necessary.

STARS Dog: This acronym describes behaviors a dog may exhibit. This acronym is used to describe dogs that are shy, timid, aloof, reserved, or skittish. These dogs can be untrusting of strangers and may become Roaming Dogs if they go missing.

Start Protocol: The routine we use to start a tracking dog on a trail or a scent scan.

Stolen Dog: Any dog that is removed from its property or the property of its owner without the owner's permission. The removal can be from real property or personal property such as a vehicle.

Stray or Stray Dog: Any dog that is off its property or the property of its owner is considered stray. This is the primary determiner when someone finds a dog. If they found the dog off its property, then it is legally considered stray. If they recovered or took the dog from, on or in the property of its owner, then the dog is generally considered stolen.

Subject Missing Dog: Term describing the dog we are looking for. Also known as Subject Lost Dog.

Tracking Dog: This is a term we use with the public for all scent detection dogs. In fact a tracking dog is actually a dog that tracks footstep for footstep. Some people feel some tracking dogs may actually follow the trail of broken ground left by the subject as it walked through. This has not been our experience, however. We generally refer to all scent detection dogs as tracking dogs as that is how the general public refers to them.

Trailing Dog: This dog follows the scent trail within fifteen to twenty feet of the actual trail. Most of our dogs follow the scent trail when close to the actual trail in this way.

Unique Identifier: Describes an aspect, physical marking, or descriptor that our missing dog has or is wearing. A unique identifier might be a specific color or marking, a specific collar, a tattoo, or other feature that is unique to that dog. Unique identifiers are generally not released to the public as we hold that information back to assist in confirming or negating sightings, leads, and clues.

Xenophobic or Xenophobia: A deep rooted fear of strangers. Extreme fear and distrust, of anything perceived to be foreign, different or unfamiliar. In our context this fear is usually of human strangers but can be related to other objects or incidences.

Resources

Companion Website to this book: http//www.howtofindalostdog.org/

As a purchaser of this book, you are eligible to participate in the companion website. The website includes additional tips, suggestions, and photos. Many of the techniques are explained in greater detail with additional photographic instructions not possible in this book.

In addition, you can submit a query form about your lost dog and the missing event surrounding his disappearance should you want professional assistance.

To log in, simply click on this photo, which is prominent on the website. To submit a query form to Karin, you will need your receipt # or date of purchase for this book.

Professional Assistance

Karin TarQwyn: http://k9pi.com/

Lost Pet Professionals: https://www.lostpetprofessionals.com/

There are additional references and resources at http://www.howtofindalostdog.org/additional-refer-ences---resources.html.

Acknowledgments

Certainly one cannot live and love the life I have without the assistance and input from others. Below are some of the people who have assisted me and/or made an impact in some way over the years in my work, research, and life.

Angie Rutherford—Private investigator, LPP partner, K9 handler, friend and many other capacities that hold this ship together. Thanks Angie.
Chris Doyle—my son, cheerleader, and holder of the greater truths. Thank you for your assistance with this book.
Mom and Dad- Although we live miles apart, my heart is still in California. Thank you.
Rob Dwinnell—You said I could do anything and I believed you.
Steve and Clare Gallizioli—You showed me a life with animals was normal and possible.
Debra Speakes—We chased wild horses as children, and as an adult you convinced me I should write a book.
Brenda Myers—Dog rescuer extraordinaire
Mark Tillinger—Friend, supporter and K9 Handler at heart
Theresa DeMatteo Tillinger- Friend, supporter, professional liaison. Thank you for your assistance with this book.
Mimi Applegate Elder- Rescuer and big time supporter. Thank you for your assistance with this book.
Jordina Thorp—K9 handler and friend
Donna Badger—Dog rescuer, responsible for rescuing many of the dogs on our K9 teams. On behalf of all... Thank you Donna.
Cindy Silverstein—K9 handler and friend
Bonnie Folz—Lost-animal advocate and expert
Chris Boyer—National Association for Search and Rescue – Made understanding scent work a breeze
Harry Charalambous—Animal-rights advocate and friend. Thank you for your assistance with this book.
Denny Adams—Dakota Territory Search Dogs. I would have never stayed with it had you not encouraged me to ignore the group and trust my dog.
Dr. Mike O'Banion, DVM—Cade's physician, the only vet he trusts.
Dr. James Gigstad, DVM
The staff at Arbor Valley Animal Hospital
Dr. Kristin Bohling, DVM
Vizsla Stealth—Ann, Mimi, Becky, and the rest of the group, you are awesome
Brenda Basiley: P.I. and K9 Profiler. Thank you for your assistance with this book.
Janeal Domenico - Wag N Train Terrier Rescue – Rescuer to the many - both human and canine.

About the Author

Karin TarQwyn is a K9 handler and licensed private investigator with more than a decade of experience tracking down missing pets. In that time, she's developed a unique and effective missing-dog recovery process based on behavior, missing event, as well as techniques specific to the situation a missing dog is most likely experiencing. Her work and techniques have been featured on CNN, PBS, and numerous other high-profile media outlets.

When not at home in Nebraska, TarQwyn travels with her K9 Team reuniting missing dogs and their families across the United States.

Bibliography

This book is a culmination of my findings and experience in the missing pet industry over the past 14 years. The profiling and analysis process is an adaptation from those techniques commonly known and used by law enforcement and to a lesser degree in Search and Rescue. The techniques and activities outlined are those that I feel to be the most effective as suggested for each scenario. Some of the techniques may be common and customary and have been used by others in the search for missing people and pets. Most of the techniques are of my own design or adaptation for the specific purpose of locating and recovering a missing dog.

The following are some of the references and sources that I have found to be helpful or have influenced me as I sought to develop the investigative processes found in this book and implemented by my investigative agency.

Berns, Annalisa, and Landa Coldiron. *Lost Cat Recovery Guide*. Sun Valley, CA: International Pet Detectives, 2010.

Boyer, Chris. Scent Work NASAR Conference, Private Publish, 2000.

Bulanda, Susan. *READY the Training of the Search and Rescue Dog*. Portland, OR: Doral Publishing, 1994.

Haglund, William D., and Marcella H. Sorg. *Forensic Taphonomy: The Postmortem Fate of Human Remains*. New York: CRC Press, 1996.

Koester, Robert J. *Lost Person Behavior*. Charlottesville, VA. DBS Productions, 2008.

Levitus, Daniel et al, *Animal Behavior*, 2009.03.18

McDougall, Len. *The Encyclopedia of TRACKS & SCATS*. Guildford, CT: The Lyons Press, 2004.

Pearsall, Milo D., and Hugo Verbruggen. *SCENT Training to Tracks Search and Rescue*. Loveland, CO: Alpine Publications, 1982.

Pet Hunters International, Kat Albrecht MAR Technician Presentation. Fresno, Ca. 2005.

Rebman, Andrew, Edward David, and Marcella H. Sorg. *Cadaver Dog Handbook, Forensic Training and Tactics for the Recovery of Human Remains*. New York: CRC Press, 2000.

Syrotouk, William G. *Scent and the Scenting Dog*. Mechanicsburg, PA: Barkleigh Productions, 2000.

Photo Credits

All photos were contributed by and are the property of Karin TarQwyn with the exception of:

Dog Captured in Trap and Sign on Stake—Angie Rutherford

Made in the USA
Monee, IL
26 April 2020